In the Wake of a Dream

Lisa Hopper

Lisa Hopper

In The Wake
Of A Dream

A True Story

TUCSON, ARIZONA

Library of Congress Cataloging-in- Publication Data
Hopper, Lisa Marie 1961-
In the Wake of a Dream
   1.   Dreams-Humanitarian aid-   2. Chicago- personal
      narratives

   I.   Title

ISBN: 978-0-9679194-0-9

Printed in the United States of America
First Paper Edition of Complete Text

TUCSON, ARIZONA

Editor: Cliff Carle
Cover Design by: Holly Romero and Nick Deak
Reviews by: Laurie Ross

This book is dedicated to my Mother, Julia Callas

Acknowledgements

So many have played a part in the accomplishment of this book and the success of World Care but, more importantly, giving credence to a dream. I would like to acknowledge all the volunteer, donors and staff that continue to make World Care a dream come true. You inspire me everyday as to the reason I am here.

I thank my family, Mom, Peter, Dad, Stephanie, Cathy and Pam. My friends, Cheryl, Ruth, Frannie, Janet (s), Nick, Nicky, Laurie, Lec, Holly, Brother, Sister, all those in Tucson and back home in Chicago for their continued support and unconditional love.

Most of all, I want to thank Rhonda for her years of patience, devotion and inspiration.

PART ONE

CHAPTER ONE

Thursday August 25, 2005

"Lisa, its Dr. Ecchiverri. We are going to start now. Are you comfortable? This is a very risky surgery, but I'm confident that all will go well. It will take two days to complete. First we will map the vessels, and tomorrow we will do the final surgery."

I kissed my mom. I told her I loved her. I told her not to worry about me.

"Doc, can we go over the plan one last time?" I asked again, feeling that if I reminded him it would somehow improve the odds of success.

I sensed that challenges such as my aneurysm had been placed in my path for reasons I had yet to learn, and I wondered what they were. The answers would come soon enough, I thought. Feeling doubtful was not an option. Having any expectation can limit options and outcomes, I reminded myself. I was aware of a pattern in my life that many of my greatest professional accomplishments occurred parallel to huge personal challenges.

In my waning moments of consciousness, I also reminded

myself that risk is a necessary part of life. Laugh often, love many, pay attention to your dreams, and never stop learning. Take chances and dare to live, I told myself. Three days shy of my 44th birthday, I thanked God for everything. Then I thought is this it? Is this all there is?

I peered into the surgical room hoping that the team of masked nurses and healthcare professionals were seasoned at their craft. What if I wake up and have half a brain missing or -can't speak or I'm blind. Even worse, what if I don't wake up at all? I have to wake up. Not to mention my family will be annoyed if I don't come out of this. I noticed how cold it was in the room as I was being gently lifted, accepted and placed onto the operating table.

"I will do my best," Dr. Ecchiverri assured me.

All I needed was to know that he felt confident about how he was going to perform that day. I thought about Mom and how I couldn't disappoint her by not making it through this, as if I had a choice in the matter. I had lived a great life full of emotion and color, but I didn't feel I'd finished yet.

"You are going to feel drowsy. Can you start counting backwards from ten?"

I began slipping out of consciousness. As I lay on the operating table I felt calm staring at the tiles on the ceiling and at the large light that canopied my body. I made no pact with God. I simply accepted that what was meant to be would be, and reminded myself that I had no regrets. I was thankful for all of the incredible lessons God had already given me in this lifetime. My vision had expanded to inspire people wanting to help others.

Then a long tunnel appeared, and events started flashing in front of me. I was still trying to count backwards.

CHAPTER TWO

Humble Beginnings

Harvey was the perfect mix between a big city and a small town. The residential streets were lined with oak, elm, and maple trees just like the big city downtown. Purple lilac bushes grew wild in most yards, and the houses were small and uniform, but unique in their own ways. We lived in a pinkish-tan shingled house with a dramatic pitched roof that peaked near a small attic window. Our kitchen window overlooked a large maple tree that canopied the backyard and led to the detached garage and our prized alleyway. Growing up, the small yard was huge and adventures abounded.

Though we were located right on the outskirts of South Chicago, my reality was that of 1960's starter homes. Oil barrel garbage cans lined the alleyways and the good old Alderman's Drug store. I saw the dramas of Chicago in the late 60's on television, but stepping outside into my peaceful neighborhood, the inner-city of Chicago seemed a world away to my seven-year-old mind.

Cattails moved freely in the wind on the gravel pathways like waving fans in a stadium as my sisters and I strolled down to go home from school. The smell of burning leaves permeated the air in fall, the smoke of barbeques in spring. Everyone in the community took pride in their property, however modest. It was our home and safe haven.

Mom kept busy at home tending to the day to day chores of raising three active girls. No sooner would we step one foot into our back yard and Mom would yell out the window,

"Come on girls we have chores to do. No lollygagging, supper will be ready by five and your Dad will be home tonight."

With no hesitation we all sprinted to the door knowing there were cookies waiting inside for us to devour after we completed our daily tasks.

Mom was a strong and determined woman early on knowing that one day we would need to take care of ourselves. She taught us things in our little lives about responsibly. Dad, a social gadfly with a taste for travel, would come home from his work trips and relax in the living room in front of the T.V. My father would pile all of us kids into the car; Stephanie, my older sister with whom I played and fought daily and my dear twin sister Cathy, to visit with relatives on weekends. I've always been very close to my twin. Mom told me that when we were two years old I used to rock my crib across the room to Cathy's, grab her by the diaper, and pull her into my crib with me. Cathy and I always stuck together. By the time I was ten, my mother became pregnant with my youngest sister Pamela.

By the late sixties no one was ignorant to the violence, crime and Mafia activity that came with the joys of living on the Southside. It was a time of war in Vietnam, Richard Nixon, Harry Kissinger, Martin Luther King and the peace demonstrations, desegregation and riots. Tensions continued to mount; it became very difficult for my parents to raise us girls in our community.

Adults weren't the only ones in conflict. Children, acting out their parents' aggressions, fought often, and gangs were everywhere. Rival schools were geographically close, so it wasn't unusual to find students from nearby schools fighting during lunch. I couldn't understand why people, especially kids my own age, were so angry all of the time. To me everyone seemed the same. My elementary school had a mixture of black and white children. It didn't take long for me to realize that the differences between people were not due to their skin color, rather due to whether they made good or bad choices in life. Despite this very logical belief system, the world around me had a much different view of good and bad. Protection of oneself came first and understanding why you needed to came later.

Even though there were radical changes in our community, I learned to adapt. Somehow I felt relatively safe growing up in Harvey. I knew my neighbors and they looked out for me. They were my contingency plan if things went wrong. I never really had to worry until faced with a problem. Neighbors watched out for each other back then, despite racial differences.

School never came easily to me because I had a hard time learning how to read. My second grade teacher once asked me to spell the word "Indian" on the blackboard. Then she left the classroom. I had no idea how to spell the word and was embarrassed to be put on the spot. Nevertheless, I approached the blackboard and proceeded to draw an Indian, hoping to gain partial credit for my attempt. Upon returning, the teacher saw my drawing and exploded. She yelled at me, and further humiliated me by spanking me in front of the entire class.

Thankfully, the incident prompted Mom to start reading with me every day. She made me repeat words over and over

5

until I got them right. Eventually, I was able to read at the same level as everyone else in my class. Before I knew it, I was reading short stories, magazines, road signs, cereal boxes…everything! I was reading out of fear, not pleasure. I was scared to be humiliated at the blackboard in front of my classmates again. I helped Cathy with her reading skills, and soon we were both improving in school.

Cathy wasn't the social type at all in school. I, on the other hand, was frequently sent to the principal's office for talking too much in class. I loved to chat and make people laugh. The pace and structure of the classroom bored me, and teachers grew frustrated with my endless questions about why things were the way they were. Teachers had a lot more room to discipline children back then, and I spent many weekday afternoons clapping erasers on the fire escape as punishment. If I were a child today, I probably would've been misdiagnosed as having ADHD and given mind-altering drugs. Fortunately, I was left to my own moorings.

Although times were difficult and my family was limited financially, I didn't know what we were missing because nobody else had much either. Instead of collecting toys, we were creative, making up our own games until dark, or until Mom called us in for dinner. The alleys were great places for hide and seek. The fields on the way to school became the African Serengeti, full of lions and rhinoceros hiding around every corner. In those days, parents ruled the house, but until dusk, kids ruled the streets.

Dad worked for the airline and would bring home old tickets and pads of paper so we set up a make-believe travel agency. We pretended to explore far off corners of the world until one sister would become upset with something and the entire company would disband due to management conflicts, and the game would be over.

Dad nicknamed me "Bones" because I was tall and skinny. He wasn't around very much when we were children because he had to travel frequently for his job. When he made it home, our personalities were at odds with each other. He had little patience for my high energy personality. I was inquisitive and eager to learn how things worked, which really irked him after coming off of a long trip away from home. I climbed trees, scaled garages, built forts, saved animals, played ball with the boys and constructed things that I'd leave for Dad to find on his workbench.

At age eleven, I asked Mom for five dollars, naive to the fact that five dollars meant the difference between having food on the table and going hungry. Rightfully, Mom admonished me to work for money if I wanted it so badly. Although I didn't understand why she was angry, Mom's suggestion to get a job excited me. So off I went to find a job in town.

The streets were bustling with kids on their bikes, old men heading to the barbershop, and women window shopping for the latest appliances. I went to almost every business in the entire town of Harvey. I approached dozens of storekeepers and business owners in search of employment. After many dead ends, I landed my very first paid job - at the military recruitment office.

I was paid one dollar per day for washing windows where recruitment posters and brochures were displayed. Sometimes I made a few extra quarters from the sergeants in the office by wiping down their desks and emptying their trash. Despite the simplicity of these tasks, the job made me feel liberated from the very first day. Finally, I could provide for myself.

Throughout my early childhood years, underneath the facade of happiness I painted on my face daily, I was experiencing dreams and visions that were often disturbingly dark for a child my age. Sometimes I would dream of war, or that I was running away from somebody attacking or chasing me. When I woke up I sometimes found myself in another part of the house, or trying to climb out of the window in the basement where my sisters and I slept. I never discussed these dreams with anybody. Even if I had discussed my dreams, the likely assessment would have been that I was working out problems in my sleep that I couldn't handle in my wakened state - which seemed reasonable to me. When I got a little bit older, I started exploring creative outlets such as drawing and writing. These activities preoccupied me and gave me a valuable conduit for processing my dreams.

I never felt pressured by my family to fit into the traditional woman's role. I loved playing sports. The White Sox and the Bears were my family's sports teams. I remember visiting my grandparents on my father's side. They were staunch Cubs fans, which was an unusual trait for Southsider's, who were known to be White Sox fans. We couldn't afford to go to games, but could watch them on television if we wanted. When I was young, for me it was more fun to play than talk about baseball. I had so much energy and loved playing ball. I used to go down to the park to play with the boys.

Not a day went by that I wasn't throwing, bouncing, or catching a ball of some sort. If not on the field, I was climbing trees, and if I wasn't in a tree, I was playing kick the can. Little League was only available for boys but as I grew up I started to feel society's prejudices against women constricting me. At age nine, I wanted to play on a Little League team. I had been playing with the local kids for years and had asked my parents for a mitt for my birthday that year. I was a lefty, so it was difficult for me to borrow a mitt from a friend. I didn't have the proper equipment to play, but I had the enthusiasm and the natural athletic ability so I headed to the ballpark for try-outs.

When I got to the registration table, a woman informed me that girls could not register; it was boys-only baseball. I asked where girls could play, and she informed me that there was no girls' team. I thought for a moment before I spoke. I resolved to play with the boys. I was good enough. I asked for permission to play with the boys, but she refused. The rules should change, I thought. I knew that I could play better than half the boys on the field, but because I was a girl I was not allowed to play.

Our closest friends outside of our family were the Charles family children. Cheryl was in our class from third grade on, and she remained friends with Cathy and me throughout the rest of our childhood. Cheryl was considered our triplet. She had an older sister named Rhonda, a younger sister named Missy, and two brothers who loved making fun of us. Even though they were older it was fun to pretend that they were our real brothers since we didn't have any.

Cheryl's mom was a strong, independent woman. We used to go over to Cheryl's house after school to see her mother coming home from work each day. A responsible, self-reliant woman, she raised Cheryl and her siblings mostly on her own, but the struggle wore heavily on her. Cheryl's parents were divorced, and it was difficult for her mom to raise the children by herself with little financial support. She worked hard and then would come home and tend to the kids. She always treated us like one of her own just as Mom treated Cheryl like one of her own. This was both good and bad at times. Mom would ground me, my sister, and Cheryl all at the same time, since we were all in cahoots when causing trouble. Cheryl's family moved often, but wherever they were, Mrs. C always welcomed us in her home and treated us kindly.

As a child, I never understood what parents went through. It was only after tapping into my own struggles later in life that I realized the difficulties life holds for adults. My mother never let us in on what she was going through with my father. She sheltered us from adult issues.

As far as I was concerned, adults had all the power. As long as I had a roof over my head, clothes on my back, and food on the table, I shouldn't have any problems. At that age, I felt I shouldn't have to worry about those things, because I thought that's what parents were for. I soon discovered that life was not so easy. I had friends and classmates who lived out of a car. That was my first hardcore introduction to poverty.

It was apparent that things had changed between my parents when my little sister Pam was born. When my Grandmother died in 1969, my mother put away some money for us; she had a plan for what was to come. The money was enough to put a down payment on a house in a safe community where there was a good public school district. All of her energy went toward securing our future. We were her chief concern.

My father, on the other hand, seemed most concerned with being away from home. His method of handling things was to ignore them. He didn't keep promises to us, and I realized quickly that it was best not to make plans with him at all. We couldn't rely on him. He lacked the values that my mother had instilled in us. My dad and I seldom got along. He was never big on words and believed that children were to be seen and not heard. Every time I saw him, I was in trouble, and I wasn't a bad kid, I swear!

Shortly before I turned thirteen, my parents divorced. I knew it was going to be tough, but I felt a sense of relief because I didn't have to deal with my father's anger anymore. I didn't feel that I was deserving of all his punishments. It was a difficult time for Mom and for the rest of the family, but once Dad left, peace finally settled in our home. Even though I loved him I was angry for how he treated my mother and me; but I now realize that he had more problems than I understood at the time. It took me close to two decades to confront my father and another twenty years to let it go. Life's lessons can often take a lifetime to figure out.

My mother had become a single mom with three teenage girls in high school. My youngest sister, Pamela, was barely five years old. Mom worried that we would become exposed to a world of drugs, teen sex, pregnancy, and violence. Mostly, she feared losing control. What she didn't realize was that by this time, she had already instilled in us great strength and responsibility that would carry us through this difficult time, and would lead us throughout our careers and lives. In the meantime, we all helped out around the house and found various avenues to earn our own money. Even though mother worked three jobs to make ends meet, she always said, "A good divorce is better than a bad marriage."

Following suit with my mother and her mother before her, I felt it was important to earn my own money. In 1977, while I was still in high school, I began working for Edward Allen Publishers in Chicago, Illinois. Jim Mercone, a retired Chicago police officer and owner of the publishing house, hired me to manage the office and design paste-up advertisements. Most commercial art and lettering was done by hand back then. Every other day, I drove to Chicago to work at Edward Allen. On weekends, I worked at local restaurants, bussing tables for extra cash. I also worked after school two nights a week at the Art Corner, where my employment perks included discounted art supplies.

After school and work, I'd work on my own projects. I set up a makeshift art studio in our basement. I propped an old ping-pong table on its side and raised it with cinderblocks to create an easel, and a wooden board I found in the alley became a drawing table. I used all different mediums thanks to the Art Corner job, from pen and ink, to oil and acrylic paint, and chalk. I also started exploring black and white photography, which led to more ideas for drawing and painting. I spent so much time down there that I sometimes fell asleep sitting at the table while in the middle of a project. Creating art was a meditative experience. One evening I fell into a deep slumber and began to dream.

I am in a shack in a desert. There is a dead animal with me - a cat, monkey, or perhaps a dog. As I peer through the small window, I recognize a carnival with a towering Ferris wheel in the distance. Then I notice a woman in a blue chiffon dress standing in the doorway with my mother and two of my sisters. I paced around the shack in circles deliberating over my next move. I want to feed the dead animal on the floor, but my Mom says, "It's time to leave the cat because it's dead." The next thing I know, I am outside of the door, walking towards the carnival, still far off in the distance. When I turn to look back at the shack, there is nothing there. The shack is gone, and with it, my mother and sisters.

Suddenly I woke and began to draw. What did this dream mean? As I starred at the image I had drawn, it beckoned me to bravely leave my family behind and move forward with my own life. After eighteen years, it was time to forge my own path, and for the first time ever, I knew I had to go it alone.

CHAPTER THREE

Military Time

I felt confused about what I should be doing with my life, after high school. My interests varied so drastically that in turn, I lacked focus. I loved to draw and paint. I resolved to find a career in medical illustration. However, I quickly learned of the necessity of a medical background in order to become an illustrator. Then one day I came across the ubiquitous U.S. Army slogan in an advertisement, "Be all you can be. Join the Army." Right then, something clicked. This was the solution - the military had education programs in medicine!

If I obtained my education through the military, it would be heavily subsidized. What's more, the physical training would challenge me as an athlete, and the discipline aspect would be a cake-walk compared to growing up with my mother. My only concern was academics, since I hadn't excelled in school and doing well was a major factor in education subsidies for military. Overall, I believed that the military would satisfy my needs and make a future career in medical illustration possible.

In 1979, I signed up for the military. In that same year, women were required to score an 89 percent on the entrance examination, while men only had to score 16. Talk about an academic challenge. I prepared for the exam and passed with flying colors. I was in!

Telling my mother that I joined the Army was another story. I could tell by her face that she wasn't happy about my decision. Her plan for me was different than my own, but for the first time, my Mom kept her opinions to herself, allowing me to lead my own life.

Basic Training

I left home for the Army in the summer of 1980, arriving at Ft. McClullen, Alabama for basic training. I don't know what I'd pictured, but it certainly wasn't this. Apparently, hundreds of other people had the same idea I'd had about joining the Army. There were so many of us--some in civilian clothing, while others wore uniforms. A large group of civilians ran alongside the road singing songs to a synchronized shuffle. I felt like Southside Dorothy; where had I landed?

As I stood on the field of Ft. McClullen contemplating turning back, I remembered my Mother's words, "When you're eighteen, on your own, paying your own way, and having your own home, you can make your own rules and do whatever you want, but until then you play by my rules." Holy Cow, I was eighteen. I'd finally started on my own journey. I quickly settled into a leadership position and began to feel more at home. I became responsible for managing and overseeing a platoon of forty women.

As the TL (training leader) I was responsible for making sure my platoon was obedient, on time, handled their chores, and that they absorbed military education. Our required knowledge base included weapons training; field exercises tactical maneuvers, nuclear, biological, and chemical warfare training and testing. I was responsible for disciplining anyone who fell out of line, and I was held accountable for their bad behavior. As punishment for misbehavior within my platoon, I would be subjected to long nights standing outside in the rain, doing push ups, peeling a million or so potatoes, kitchen patrol, cleaning bathrooms, digging ditches, and running extra miles beyond the five required before 6:00am.

A few weeks into training, several platoons, including mine, marched up to the firing range with M-16's in tow. Upon arrival, we cleared the foxholes of rattlesnakes and generally tidied up the area. It was a calm afternoon until one disgruntled recruit took a shot at the Drill Sergeant and missed. After her failed attempt, she was tackled and taken away, never to be seen again. That day we all paid for her outburst. For the five hours that followed, the rest of us cleaned and dismantled weapons. When we were done, we were required to run back to the barracks with our weapons overhead. This is extremely tiring, despite our conditioning as soldiers. As always, I gave it everything I had.

I received a couple of letters from my Dad during my time in basic training. Having served in the military himself during the Korean War in the 1950's, Dad knew how lonely it becomes being away from family. He also knew how important mail call is during the end of day formation. Our relationship was strained during most of my childhood, but on the military level, we finally found some common ground. I was grateful for his encouragement, even if it took eighteen years to get it out of him.

The army was exhausting. As a result, I slept soundly and rarely dreamed. I was determined to succeed. My obedience, leadership, and fear of failure finally paid off; I was named the top female recruit in my basic training cycle. Although I longed for the comforts of home, this recognition signified my coming into adulthood. I felt liberated by this achievement and was eager for more. I wasn't fast-tracked on a road to success, but when facing obstacles, I learned to correct my own mistakes. I had the strength to forge my own future and reach my goals.

The second hurdle in the military was far more difficult than the first. We stood in formation to receive our next assignment; I wondered what the future held for me. Then I was handed my orders, "Private Hopper, you are scheduled to report to duty in San Antonio, Texas, where you will enroll in 91P10 Radiology Technology, for your first training phase. Once you complete the Field Medic course you will then proceed to the next phase of your training which is Radiology Technology." As I stood there in my pristine pressed uniform I began to wonder what happens if I don't pass the medic training.

"Private Hopper do you have any questions?"

"Well, Sergeant, what if a person fails the class?"

"You will not fail is that understood? Failure is not an option. You did not pass Basic Training to turn around and fail did you?"

"No Sergeant"

"I can't hear you Private!"

At the top of my lungs I repeated "No Sergeant".

Still in deep thought, another Drill Sergeant approached me after we broke from formation to let me know if I pass the Field Medic Training but fail at my Radiology Course then I become a field medic for four years. There is no do over, that is why you become a medic first so if you don't pass that, the Army gets to choose your destiny for your term duration. She reassured me that I should have no problem, but she never sat in a class when I was taking a test... not pretty.

"Great …. Thanks."

I had some time off before heading to San Antonio, so I headed home to Chicago to show my new figure off to my family. While in basic training I managed to gain twenty pounds of muscle and lose eighteen inches all over my body. I was strong and fit which made me feel good about myself.

I gave Mom an Army sticker to put on her car even though I was still unsure of where she stood. She hadn't been thrilled that I had joined in the first place, but before I left a few days later, I noticed the sticker displayed on the back bumper of her car. She hadn't mentioned it to me, which made my heart warm with love. I gathered some last things, got in my car, a red 1974 Mustang, and set off for the U.S. Army Academy of Health Sciences in San Antonio, Texas for training.

San Antonio, Texas

If Alabama was a culture shock compared to Chicago, San Antonio was something else entirely. Never once had I seen so much equipment focused exclusively on medical training. Radiology was one of the most extensive classes the military had to offer. Students were required to learn two jobs instead of one. First, there was field medic training, so that if the career job (91P20) didn't work out, the student would be placed as a field medic for the duration of four years. This was news to me when I entered the program; I had no plans to work as a field medic for the next four years. I excelled in field training however, and before long, I began what I was there for, radiology school. Around that time, I moved into a dorm on the top of a big hill on the military campus. At times, it felt more like college than military.

Due to an overabundance of students, a large portion of students were delayed from entering classes. My roommates and I opted to wait three months and took an opportunity to work for the First Sergeant in the meantime. He trained us in

17

parachuting and tactical maneuvers, an opportunity I jumped at, no pun intended. So maybe this wasn't like college, it was military training, even if I took it lightly at times. For three months we learned about fieldwork, military strategy, color guard training, and other challenging but necessary things.

When the First Sergeant learned that I could draw, he asked me to paint the US and Korean maps on the dayroom walls in exchange for skipping formation and wearing civilian clothes (I didn't even have to negotiate that last part). Leadership was not without heart, I thought, something I'd learned from my mother but was repeating itself in the military.

Despite the calmness of San Antonio compared to basic training, we were still being conditioned to handle long hours awake on a regular basis. Every two days, we had regular 24 hour fire guard and patrol watch. Despite my uncertainty about a career in radiology, I felt good about what I was doing. I faced challenges everyday to do things I didn't think I could, and I was able to experience failure in a way that allowed me to accept it and learn from my mistakes. I repeated errors until I learned on my own how to correct them.

Even though I was just one person, I felt like I was leading up to making an impact on the world. I was a woman in the armed forces, serving my country, and having the opportunity to be educated at the same time. Classes began with basics in calculus, physics, and electrical mechanics. Then there was anatomy and physiology for eight hours per day, five days a week. Finally, there was homework each night, and lab for five months at a time; and I thought high school was tough!

How did I do? Well, anatomy and physiology were pretty easy when I learned to visualize concepts in my head. I did a similar thing with physics. I gathered all of the equations together and redeveloped them to form a picture that I was able to apply to the equations. Once I'd figured out a way to fit it all together, the workload actually felt reasonable. It was all about putting things on my terms.

I spent a lot of time drawing body parts, bones, diseased organs, and systems. I committed these pictures to memory which helped me on exams. I systematically prepared myself for the most important tests. I learned to prioritize this way in order to make the most of limited time. I graduated from school and awaited my final orders, as I had after Phase One. I was handed my Phase II *on-the-job training* destination and I was off to a new location...New Jersey?

Unlike everyone else heading to Walter Reed in Washington D.C., I was going to Ft. Mammoth, New Jersey to begin the drive up the coast to a small hospital near the ocean. I bid my friends farewell and with my Rand McNally in hand, hopped onto the I-10 for nearly 2000 miles.

I had a lot of time to think about what I'd accomplished and where I was going along the way. Within seven months, I had become completely independent from my family and gained an education through the military, something that wouldn't have been available to me otherwise. I'd tackled many challenges along the way...getting through basic training, traveling cross-country, passing Advanced Individual Training, jumping out of an airplane, helicopter, and off of a three story building. Physically, I had gained twenty pounds and lost twelve inches all over my body. I learned sparring tactics, how to use defensive weapons, how to throw grenades and survive in the wilderness by eating snakes and bugs. For the most part, I felt good about all of these experiences, except for that last part about the bugs.

Although it was my interest in medical illustration that led me to the army, I began a career in radiology instead. I found the addition of technology to be much more fascinating

19

and challenging then drawing. There was still visualization in imaging, so my artistic skills were never dormant. I was new to the field of medicine, and had much yet to discover in this vast field of interest. As I continued to learn about my new field, I found that I had a knack for it more and more. Drawing subsequently became a learning tool for my medical studies.

My permanent duty in Washington D.C.

I served active duty in the United States Army Medical Corps from 1980 until 1984, and I was inactive for an additional two years in the Reserves. Upon completion of medical training in New Jersey (where only about fifty percent of us managed to make it through), the Army assigned me to work at Walter Reed Army Medical Center (WRAMC) in Washington, D.C. At the time, this was the largest, most technologically advanced 1200 bed medical military facility in the country. From Alabama, to Texas and on to New Jersey, Washington D.C. finally felt a lot more like home than my previous residences. Finally, I had four seasons again; city streets crowded with locals and tourists alike, and museums, theaters and subway stations, not to mention incredible restaurants! It was a melting pot of cultures and had a crime rate that challenged N.Y. At long last, a place I could call home.

When I arrived at my new duty station, many soldiers were leaving to head overseas, so our initiation was baptism by fire. Barb Conville, one of the best civilian techs in the field, took me under her wing. She led me through the bureaucratic politics and systems that come with operating in such a large facility. She was my mentor and became a close friend.

I spoke to Mom every week on Sundays but did my best to remain vague about my job. I didn't want to fail, and felt there was no middle ground between failure and success, none that my mom would understand, anyway. I needed to focus completely on the task at hand; weakness or second-guessing myself was not an option. Sharing my concerns with my mother was even less of an option. If I let my emotions out, I knew they would get the best of me. The last thing I wanted was to disappoint my mother.

Within a year I was making good rank, equating to more money and less supervision. I lived off of the base. The only housing available was Abrams Hall, which was restricted to PFC (Private First Class) and below. I was happy to live elsewhere; I wasn't especially interested in the social scene. My main focus was simply to put what I'd learned in school into practice.

Like many of the personnel, my time was divided by a multitude of tasks making up for shortness of staff and new trainees. I spent a large part of my day in radiology and forensics. My time in radiology was spent conducting X-rays on regular patients, whereas the majority of my forensics work took place in the morgue. I also worked with Armed Institute of Pathology (AFIP), performing radiology exams on everything from post mortem victims of animal experimentation to murder victims, from standard autopsies, to radiation exposures and war casualties. There were diseased body parts too, sometimes of unknown origin. Funding flowed freely in the 1980's and Reed housed state of the art technologies. Whenever something new was needed or invented, even if it was one of a kind, Reed was able to acquire it, no questions asked. As a result, I worked with new diagnostic technologies that hadn't even hit the mainstream market, and simultaneously had access to products that dated back to Roentgen's discovery of the x-ray in 1895. Physics was yet to be computerized as it is today, so a strong grasp of numbers was integral to operate successfully. The work was fascinating and endless. We regularly received unresolved cases from all over the world. Our sources ranged from organizations like NASA, FBI, CIA, NSA, Navy, to countries including Germany, even Asia. All work was completed with the utmost confidentiality.

21

Security of private information was of high priority.

Protocols, physics equations, and variables on conditions of death had to be worked out in order to solve each mystery that came across the table. This made the work very difficult but incredibly rewarding. Another lesser mentioned requirement that kept our team fairly limited in size was the need for a strong stomach. For example, on an otherwise ordinary day in the office, I remember a colleague reporting that "a floater" had come in. We were asked to go down to the morgue to inspect a new case. The pathologist had yet to arrive, but the radiologist was there and asked that we go down to the morgue and open up the bag. We didn't realize that the bag was very full as we opened it. A floater, I soon learned, was someone who had been pulled out of water. The bag was on a steel gurney. The smell was indescribable. Rotted flesh and the image of the person who it was supposed to be didn't match up. The partially decomposed and inflated body made the features completely unrecognizable, and coupled with the horrific smell, it was an awful sight. Fortunately, I have a deviated septum, which limited my sense of smell to a slight whiff. While others were dropping to their knees by the smell, I wasn't as affected. I sensed (no pun intended) that this issue with my nose proved to be quite advantageous for my career in forensics.

I was taught quickly how a little bit of Vics vapor rub helped me mask the stench of the body. Once the pathologist had arrived, X-rays were taken, which was actually quite difficult due to the amount of moisture in the tissue. The body was partially clothed and the pathologist asked me to take a remaining shoe off. When I pulled it, the entire foot came with it. "Is this supposed to do this?" I asked, holding the foot out to the pathologist. I think he expected me to faint, but I was fairly resilient. It was an equation nightmare, factoring in all of the variables in order to get a good X-ray. It was challenging because I was always mastering my techniques, and in the end, very rewarding.

We had to do our best to solve the case. Once a case was started, it had to be completed. There was no backing down, but there was a team of experts to pick apart the clues together. Knowing that I was a part of that team devoted to solving a potentially deadly problem motivated me to play as strong a role as anyone else. The endurance I'd built in the military, pulling twenty-four hour duty without shutting an eye, paid off at such times. We had our share of twenty-four hour days as deadlines on cases approached. Work was intense and thorough. During my time at Walter Reed, I assisted in approximately one hundred and fifty autopsies. Some of the most trying included pediatric radiology studies related to child abuse cases, and various animal studies for the Armed Forces Institute of Pathology.

The sleep deprivation and hectic schedule was getting to me. Another six months passed before my dreams began again. When my face hit the pillow at night, I drifted quickly into deep sleep for those few hours I could afford to stop what I was doing. As a result, I only experienced one to three dreams a year throughout most of the 1980's, but as soon as things began to settle for me professionally, the dreams returned. After completing my tour of duty in 1984, I received an honorable discharge. Though scarce at the time, the dreams I was having were as vivid and detailed as ever, illuminating a database of symbols I had yet to comprehend. Many years later, the meanings of past dreams began to reveal themselves to me.

CHAPTER FOUR

Rock Bottom

After leaving the military, I remained in Washington. I'd found a job working with a group of radiologists. My work in forensics also landed me a consulting position, setting up mobile clinics for the Navy's HANES III studies. I helped design, develop, and implement mobile trailers that would house various disciplines of medical testing. In addition, my assignments included collecting data on civilians suffering from arthritis, osteoporosis, and gout. The units and personnel traveled across the country performing exams on patients and collecting data to be assessed and used at a later date. Collecting data was the tedious part, working with a great team of doctors and engineers made the overall experience extremely rewarding.

I was promoted to managing the mobile systems, which required travel to remote parts of the US, where study sites were based. Once there, my assignment was to perform equipment systems tests, teach our procedures to new hires, conduct data management, and write reports. I was challenged to solve systemic and technical problems in the field. Although these tasks required skills in radiology, more than that, they tapped into my ability to communicate ideas to my team that could then be used to troubleshoot when I had moved on to the next site.

Around this time, I decided to continue my education in college. My years in the military had made a huge impression on me. I'd begun to carve a niche for myself in the world. I also had my hands in several different projects, never relying on a single job for security. I worked two jobs during college and found some time to do consulting on the side. Multi-tasking gave me a sense of security.

My personal life wasn't suffering, but it wasn't thriving, either. Relationships had always been challenging, since I felt fitting someone into my life would require me to give up some of my passion for my work, which wasn't in the cards for me then. As a result, most of the time I was ill-matched, but I didn't have the time to commit to anyone anyway. I had no trouble sharing myself with others, and had many friends, but deep down I felt disconnected from those around me, as if they didn't understand my way of thinking and varied interests. As a result, despite the friendships I'd made, I felt very alone. When I began community college, I again immersed myself in learning and let my desire for companionship take a back seat.

Core classes were required in order to move on to more interesting courses. I applied the same methods of study I'd learned in the military to excel in school. In anatomy class, everything became a photographic image in my brain. The same was true for physiology and physics equations. I visualized everything. I crafted detailed drawings of bones, systems, molecular structures, and algorithms, which is a sequence of instructions to solve a problem. I coupled my new study of medicine with the knowledge I'd gained in my military education, to pursue a degree in Radiology Administration and Physics.

Fear of failure also carried over from my time in the

military. To cope with this, as I had in the past, I insured myself with multiple plans, in case my original plan took an unexpected turn. After all, the original plan had included art, something which I was not yet ready to abandon.

My transcripts from the military gave me credit for some required classes at community college. I was eligible to test out of two years of college. Everything hinged on passing the National Radiology Boards which scared me to death. had always been an awful test taker. I had to find creative ways to study, as I had in the past. I needed to take the test on my terms, and I needed to pass that exam.

At night I continued to have vivid dreams. My dreams were made up of vivid images, pictures of places, people, events, and symbols, yet their meanings remained unclear. The significant dreams would not fade, and would creep into my consciousness during the day. They would grow stronger as the day went on, causing me to lose my concentration on daily tasks. Recording them in my journal took them out of my mind. I only wrote down the more prominent ones, just in case. In case of what, I didn't know.

Shortly after I finished my military duty, I settled down a bit and for investment, I purchased another home with a partner. Everything seemed to be going smoothly. I had to pass the National Registry Board examination, a requirement for the present position I held at Washington Radiology.

It was the end of 1985. I failed round one of my national boards by a few points, but was optimistically awaiting the results of round two, when suddenly my world came crashing down. Not only had I already officially failed the exam once, I found that my business partner had sold our home, taken all our money, and left with no forwarding address. Fortunately, I was able to move back into a condo that I had purchased as an investment several years earlier. Two days later the storm resumed when I received notice from the National Registry that I had failed the radiology boards for the second time. The margin was even worse; I'd failed by seven points. When word of my failure quickly traveled to Washington Radiology, I lost my job. I was a bad test taker, but I was good at my job, I thought. I began second-guessing myself and my career. As the holiday season approached, my life was snowballing out of control.

I flew back to Chicago for Christmas only to get into a fight with my family, which given my current state, came as no surprise to me. I didn't speak to them for the next three months. I arrived back in Washington D.C. just as my personal shit storm had given way to a regional snowstorm. During my drive home from the airport, I blew two piston rods out of the side of my engine which left me with no car. When I finally arrived at my condo, I went through the mail and found that I had been sent a $6,000 property tax bill for the house that my ex-partner had stolen from me! As if things couldn't get any worse, while I was out of town, my cat had dug up all of the dirt from every single houseplant, and shredded every roll of toilet paper that she could find. Granted, the cat thing wouldn't have been much to complain about had it been an isolated issue, but in the scheme of things, it was the icing on the cake.

Despite my troubles, I believed that the military would be able to help me out of this situation with a job until I could get my career back in working order. In February 1986, I traversed the cold to my soon to be new, old job at Walter Reed. After filling out the DD-171 form, I was able to resume my position as Head of Fluoroscopy at the hospital. Over the next few months, I made a commitment to passing that damn Radiology exam. It would be my third and final attempt. I disciplined myself to study Selman's Book of Physics, the bible of radiology physics, as well as to review my anatomy and physiology books for five hours every night. After a full day of work at the hospital, I'd eat, give my cat some love, and settle in to study until midnight. My test date was scheduled for that summer.

Three months passed quickly and the looming test date became a reality. The morning of the exam, to calm my nerves, I downed two canned piña coladas that I had purchased at a local liquor store. I threw my fate into the hands of the universe, albeit a slightly drunken, tropical universe, and prayed that I would pass this time around.

PART TWO

CHAPTER FIVE

The Fine Art of Juggling

Washington D.C. 1986

The morning air was heavy with mist and a threat of rain hovered over the city. As I took off for my morning run along Sligo parkway on the Maryland side, I began thinking of my military days and the cadence of song we sang while taking each stride. Today could be the day that it comes in the mail. They said it would arrive around now. The physical exercise helped me stay grounded and take my mind off of any negative thoughts that always wanted an opportunity to come in. My body began to heat up after the first mile and the sun was desperately eager to shine light on what started out to be a gloomy morning. I knew that the mail carrier came early on Saturday so I paced myself to take a sprint on the last leg of my four mile. With sweat beading my brow I was determined to stay focused on the positive. After all the work I had done to pass the test and failing it twice, I simply did not want to start over; I just had to pass it. I did not want to think about the "what if". With my heart racing and my gait holding a solid rhythm, I turned the corner of the heavily tree lined street just blocks from my condo. As my eyes scanned the damp streets with cars close together, I saw the mail truck heading for my building. My chest began to tighten as my body wanted to stop and slow to avoid the possible disappointment. It was one of those moments were everything flashed in front of me. Everything I had worked for since I left Chicago when I was just eighteen to join the military. First you're 18 then in just seconds you're 26.

I finally reached the beginning of the driveway. The mail carrier was already out of her truck and was quickly placing the mail in each of the boxes. I stop and grabbed my knees to brace my pained legs and catch my breath. I wanted to desperately stay in medicine. For the last eight years it had become my passion, my confidence and a part of who I wanted to be. I waited patiently as she closed the mailbox. I pulled out my key. Could this be the day that defines the rest of my future - or would this be the day I would have to rethink what I thought was my destiny?

I approached the box and placed the key in the hole. Just then, the sun began to glisten on the wall. I grabbed the stack of envelopes and thumbed through them one by one. Then, one thin envelope addressed to Ms. Lisa Hopper R.T. appeared. My heart was racing with anticipation when I tore it open. As I held my breath, the results of my exam appeared. I had passed with nearly a perfect score! As I stood starring at the letter I could hardly believe it. I looked to the sky and thanked the heavens, and then I let out a sound that made a dog turn and duck about a half a block away. I began to cry.

Over the next three years I worked in radiology as a technologist as well as painting and selling my art. I worked as many hours as I could fit into my schedule to get back on track. By 1988 I was well on my way to digging myself out of the hole I had managed to bury myself in. I had managed to land a good paying technologist job at a hospital just minutes from my condo.

Everything was getting back on track. Having my National Certification made me feel validated and justified. It was time to get back in school. I decided to pick up a couple of classes at the local community college and work on finishing my degree.

One of the classes was creative writing. The professor was a young woman who had a degree in English and History. As the bell rang at the end of day one, she announced our first assignments:

"Class I want you to write an essay about your family and someone who has inspired you in some way."

After work, I headed to the library to pick up books to learn how professional writers wrote about other people, and to get an understanding of how to interpret what I wanted to say. I realized early on I was a much better speaker than a writer. What I didn't realize at the time was how important this little story would be to my future.

"Mom, I have started a writing class. The assignment is about writing our family history. I didn't know much about the genealogy of our family, so I thought I would call to see if you could enlighten me. Can I ask you a couple of questions?"

"Well, it depends, like what?"

"Grandma Spolar, your mom. Did she come over on the boat from Europe? And how did we get to Chicago?"

Once she found out it wasn't about her directly, she was eager to reminisce and talk about the past. The previous family history I had gotten was from my older sister who claimed we were French, but when Mom began to talk this was very far from what I had thought was our heritage. I was curious to see if we had any doctors or medical people in our family, or maybe military, perhaps that would explain my interests and shed some light about me as a person.

Mom took a big breath and let out a long, drawn out sigh. I pulled out a pen to take notes and came up with my first homework assignment.   After the long Sunday conversation with Mom, we hung up and I began typing:

My Grandma Mary was born in the cold winter of 1904 in Pennsylvania to two immigrants from the Balkans. They had traveled to the New World separately by boat and landed at Ellis Island when they were both around 16 years old.   As a child, Mary's mother, Bara Radovic from Horvat, Croatia met Mathias Stegner, both born in the late 1870's, and emigrated from Goleck, Austria through Breman, Germany. They married and settled down in Pittsburg, Pennsylvania. After fathering seven children and working as a laborer for many years, Mathias died suddenly in his mid-thirties. The cause of death was never determined.

Bara was a true believer in the Catholic Church until her poverty-stricken husband needed to be buried. She went to the church where she prayed and gave her weekly earnings. An anonymous gift came in to have him buried in the Catholic cemetery, but the church did not allow him to be buried there because the family had not given enough money to the church. He was buried in Potter's Field with no grave stone, an unrecognized soul of God. From that day forward Mara only put her faith in God and not in churches or priests.

Great Grandma Radovic had no money and spoke very little English, which made it difficult for her to find a job. So she could feed her children, the siblings were sent to work. Grandma Mary was sent to the Spolar family at the age of 12 to work in their boarding house as a chambermaid. The Spolars lived in Dixmoor, Illinois, a suburb on the south side of Chicago. They owned a boarding house, where, in return for food and a place to stay, Grandma cooked and cleaned for the boarders who worked on the B &O railroad. Grandma Mary was in love with Stephan Krukrek, a Yugoslavian sculptor, but old man Spolar did not want to lose his laborer who had grown into a beautiful woman, so he coerced Grandma to marry his son Rudy who was also in love with someone else. They quickly had children. Stephanie, the oldest, died of rheumatic fever at the age of 12, which put Grandma into a deep depression. Despite my Grandfather Rudy's attempt to be happy with the arrangement, after the loss of his first child, he began to struggle with alcoholism. He died of consumption at the age of 42, leaving Grandma to tend to three children, my mother Julia, and my uncles, Frank and Rudy Jr. After Grandpa Rudy's death, Grandma continued to work for Old Man Spolar. Though the Spolar house was intolerable, it was the only family she knew.

Mom was ten when she lost her father. After he died, old man Spolar became meaner than ever. Mom started working in the boarding house with Grandma, cooking and cleaning. Mom cooked before school for the boarders and then walked several miles to attend class for the day. She returned home to more chores until bedtime.

Old man Spolar continued to make Grandma and Mom's lives miserable until his death in 1945. For the first time in my mother's life she received a new dress to attend his funeral.

After Spolar's death, the boardinghouse life began to change. Grandma, with her short spoken comments laid the goals for her daughter: "Now Julia, my dear daughter, you will go to school and get an education, learn to type and become a secretary. You can make your own money and have a successful career and take care of your own problems."

Starring at her mother with big brown eyes she obediently responded, "Yes Mother, of course I will".

Grandma reconnected with her old flame, Stephan.

Stephen was quite an accomplished sculptor and had returned to the US after having worked on the Vatican in Europe. However, despite his accomplishments, Stephan had little money, so he moved into the boarding house to be with Grandma.

Mom had managed to become quite liberated and self-confident despite the constant mental abuse she had endured with old man Spolar, as well as Stephan, who had picked up where he left off. After high school she and several other girls got jobs working at AT&T Phone Company on South Water Street in Chicago. Her life was changed forever as she began to make her own money and experience what life had to offer.

One evening, Julia returned home from work to find her mother crying in her bedroom. "What's wrong, Mother?" she asked as she approached the half opened door. "Its Stephan, he is very sick." "Sick...? Oh no." "I'll need for you to help a little more around here." "Of course Mother." With that said, Julia continued to work but also made time to take care of things at the house.

After a painful battle with throat cancer, Stephan died and Grandma was alone again to tend to her boarders. By then Julia was seriously dating Bill Hopper a local metal worker. In 1959 they married and quickly started a family-and that's where we come in.

On weekends, Mom would pack us up to go to Grandma's house. We called it "Grandma's place" but everybody else called it "Mary's place." The boarding house was filled with steel mill workers and gypsies who found their way to her tavern adjacent to the living quarters. Grandma had the corner lot, and the house was separated into small rooms for boarders to sleep, a kitchen, a large dining room, and a run-down bar area with a juke box that played 45's. The juke box was my favorite part of "Grandma's place." We listened to Tom Jones, *Delilah* and Frank Sinatra,

Strangers in the Night, and *Release Me* by Englebert Humperdink.

My sisters and I played mostly in the courtyard when we weren't helping out around the house. Grandma had a generous spirit and took in practically any person who had problems and needed help. She was a soft-spoken, tiny woman with a big heart, but like my mother, Grandma yielded a heavy hand if anyone in her presence needed straightening out.

As we piled out of the car every Saturday morning, Grandma would hand us our chores. There was always work to be done. The smell of ammonia lingered everywhere. She was constantly cooking and shuffling across the floor. Somehow, Mom made sweeping, mopping, washing pots and pans, and cleaning bathrooms fun. While we worked, we played hide and seek. We'd often hear a van pull up outside, and we'd drop what we were doing to meet the sausage delivery man. He'd greet us time and again with smiles, free sausages, and tortillas.

A man named Tony, a young gypsy border, would help us with our chores while he sat at the bar. He pulled me way up high on his shoulders so that I could clean the top of the bar. I was always surprised to find quarters when I swept up there, and Grandma let me keep them. It never occurred to me that either she or Tony had placed those quarters there. However, cleaning the top of the bar was not without risk, despite the good chance of reward. I remember plenty of times when I blindly patted my hand to sweep away dust, only to find creepy cockroaches squirming around. This was a reminder that Grandma's house was old and had been infested with these disgusting little creatures for years and years. *No* amount of ammonia helped our cause.

Mom taught us that if we worked hard we would always have a job and be able to take care of ourselves. I learned at an early age not to ask for handouts, to be thankful for what I was given however small, and to make the best of what we'd been given. My mother's advice helped me to be creative with whatever resources were available. So when Grandma offered us an old box and a spoon and said, "Go play," my sisters and I would find a million things to do with that spoon and box, occupying us for hours on end. Grandma's gifts encouraged us to use our imagination and improvisational skills – some of the greatest gifts within ourselves that are all too often overlooked.

Grandma never stopped, even when it was obvious to others that she was too old to be working so hard. Grandma began to suffer from severe heart disease and diabetes which caused her a great deal of pain, but she never complained. Mom would have to sit Grandma down to tend to her diseased limbs. She'd wrap Grandma's legs in cloth to stop the oozing of her ulcerated calves from the years of standing while she worked. Then she'd bathe her, cook for her, and tend to her needs. In 1969, when I was in third grade at John G. Whittier School in Harvey, Illinois, Grandma Spolar died. Finally, her work was done. After her death we went back to what used to be Mary's Place only to find the boarding house run down and infested with vermin. Weeds had grown in the once robust flower-lined courtyard. Grandma's Place was on the "condemned" list by the city.

These were the hardships my family had endured. They weren't from royalty or a lineage of military generals, they were hardworking people who suffered from life's unexpected twists and turns. They were God's perfect imperfections.

When I turned the paper in, the teacher asked to see me after class. I was hoping it was going to be good news but I was not confident. After class I approached her desk.

"Well, you wanted to see me?

"Yes." as she pulled my paper from the pile. "Lisa, I don't want to discourage you but I don't think this is your best writing.

I know you can do better. I'm giving you a B. I know you worked hard at this, but at this rate, you will never be a literary master."

I had to come back with something, so I said, "I guess it's a good thing that I'm in Radiology with little words and lots of numbers."

I left the class with a passing grade and a better understanding of my family and what I was not very good at. Regardless of what she said I was thrilled at getting a B, and at the time "literary master" wasn't even a part of my vocabulary.

I arrived home to find a message on my machine. I had signed up with a Temp agency to take extra work in the evening and weekends to earn extra money.

"Hello Lisa, this is Sharon at First Assist. Can you work the graveyard shift at George Washington University on K Street this Saturday? They need coverage for two nights in the Emergency Room."   George Washington University Hospital was know amongst the Tech's as, "Saturday night knife and gun club" with everything and anything coming in from the drug wars and high murder rate of D.C. It was also known for taking care of our nation's political leaders such as Ronald Reagan in 1981 with a gunshot wound, George Bush, Chief Justice William Rehnquist, Dick Cheney and Larry King. Even though he is not a political leader he is famous in his own right.   "I wonder who I'll see rolling in and be taking care of during the wee hours of the night?"

CHAPTER SIX

George Washington University

By 1989 I had gained a tremendous amount of experience in the radiology field. After working the two nights as a temporary tech for George Washington University Medical Center, they hired me immediately as an emergency room technologist. There was an initial two-week probationary period at GWUMC, after which the department administrator asked me to come on full time. I gladly accepted the job and all of its perks, the best getting a pro bono education at George Washington University.

Within three months, at the age of twenty-eight, I became the technical manager of the Radiology department. My goal in this position was to improve the department so that it would run like a well-oiled machine. Ironically, my former academic nemesis, physics, became my closest ally in my efforts to decipher smoother methods of operational practice. Using physics, I was able to sketch home-grown equations in my head and apply these equations to current processes. This granted me an entirely new perspective of human adaptability and expectations.

I found a parallel existed between the principles behind the laws governing the protection and prevention of radium loss and the management of employees with varying skill sets. By applying this scientific formula to the workplace, I found that this analogy would help to decrease redundant personnel while simultaneously increasing the quality of service. Understanding how electricity, capacitors, circuitry, molecules, and electrons worked, and how these principles of physics could be applied, enabled me to recognize necessary improvements in the workplace that had been overlooked. Physics made it easier for me to consider and predict how changes would affect my department's performance.

My superiors challenged me to cut my staff by one third, to increase productivity, and to bring the department out of the red, all while maintaining employee approval. Despite the high level of difficulty in carrying out this balancing act while making improvements, I truly found enjoyment in the challenge--putting my problem-solving skills to the test to not only meet, but exceed these expectations.

While running the department at GWUMC, I procured five research grants, taught several classes in the application of radiology in forensics, and continued to travel around the country doing assessments for the HANES III mobile medical research projects. Along the way, I developed a forensic radiographic computerized technique that proved useful in identifying human remains. As the innovator of this procedure, I had the privilege of working on many high-profile cases. I had a predictive dream about the nature of the body of work I was about to embark on.

May 16, 1992

It seemed as though I was traveling to many different places, but every new place felt familiar. It was as if I had been there before. I remember standing alongside to observe the action, as if a theatrical production were going on before me. As the curtain rose, different scenarios presented themselves to me. There were old homes and businesses.

Four skulls and skeletons appeared to be hanging on display. It appeared we were in an old school building surrounded by a fence. Stone carved statues and sandstone miniatures lined the front of the building. There was another image in which a skull lay in the back of a small house. The teeth and jaw of the skull were very prominent. Then I saw a big elephant, walking down the street before crossing at an intersection.

A couple of months later, there was brief message on my answering machine from Dr. David Hunt, a forensic anthropologist at the Smithsonian Museum of Natural History.

Before I had a chance to return the call, and as I sat in my closet-sized office, a young man wearing a plaid shirt and blue jeans knocked on my wall.

"Hi. Are you Lisa Hopper?"

"Yes".

"You have quite a reputation around here."

"I'm not exactly sure how to take that and you are?"

"I'm Dave Hunt... umm, Dr. David Hunt from the Smithsonian. Dr. Davis sent me to talk to you about a project that he said you would be able to help with."

"Yes, he does that a lot." I shrugged. "How is it that I can help you?"

"We need help with the technical evaluation of some ancient remains," he said earnestly, "but have no idea where to start."

"I'm not sure I have the time to do this," I frowned.

"What can I do to persuade you?"

As I turned to look at the piles of work on my desk the

answer was simple: "Well, groveling may be involved and coffee with cream, no sugar."

"Ok," he smiled, "I think that would be manageable."

After two hours of discussion we had a general plan to evaluate the Peruvian and Egyptian mummies. Dr. Hunt's laid-back and gentle demeanor was a warm welcome to the hustle and bustle of a busy inner city hospital and a fresh layer of sarcasm made the work even more fun. Several days later Dave brought the mummies over to the hospital. We met up with a Radiologist and drove over to the lab.

"Watch the face!" Hunt warned his assistant Alex, who was unknowingly resting his arm on the sarcophagus as the van took off.

"These remains were discovered in Luxor Egypt and named after the minister of Turkey who donated them to the Smithsonian in 1886," Dave explained to me.

My participation to help interpret and preserve the historical past of ancient times was a once in a lifetime creative challenge. Our collaboration involved the use of modern day imaging technology to actuate the diagnostic testing needed to determine cause of death. As our research advanced, new technologies and methods were needed and our team was expected to create and implement new technologies along the way. In order to see inside the wrapped mummies and one sarcophagus without becoming too invasive, I developed some creative shadowing techniques and a three-dimensional computerized autopsy to help maintain the integrity of the preserved mummy.

After several months, Dr. Hunt educated me on the deterioration processes of tissue and bone as they come into contact with various soils, weather elements, and resins.

Thousands of bones at our disposal allowed us to examine various preservation techniques used around the world according to different religions, regions, climates, and cultures. He assigned some relevant readings on the decomposition of bodies by larva, rats, beetles, lice, and any other squirmy creature imaginable. The work and research was fascinating and I was hooked. Eighteen hour days came and went quickly and I was eager to learn more.

Dr. Hunt and I began to develop a close friendship through our shared love of forensics. Hours would pass while perusing a specimen without us even realizing we hadn't spoken to each other. I felt contentment that he was there. His kindness and sense of humor allowed me fortitude.

My team was challenged with a call from Italy after our ground-breaking work with the mummies. There was a discovery of human remains lying in a pool of ice, half exposed to sun and weather, high in the mountains on the Austrian-Italian border. Apparently, the Austrians had found the body and assuming foul play, pressured the Italian authorities to excavate it. Oblivious to what they had found, the Italian officials took very little care in removing the remains from the icy ground. Once fully excavated, the remains were brought down from the preserving coldtemperature to a non-climate controlled room.

Photos of the remains were sent to us. At first glance, we assumed the pictures were out of focus, but it soon became clear that the photos weren't blurred, the body was. A large fungus was growing rapidly on the bones and remaining tissue, causing the entire specimen to appear fuzzy. Per our insistence, the body was moved immediately to a refrigerated container to slow the fungus formation, affording more time to evaluate the discovery. A carbon-dating study determined that the remains were over 5,000 years old!

"Clearly," Dr. Hunt commented with a smile, "no suspects will be rounded up, and no arrests are imminent." The clothing and tools found on the specimen were also tested. As soon as this information had been announced to the scientific community, an international forum was created to manage what became known as "The Iceman's" preservation and to delegate ownership.

Our subsequent work on the Peruvian mummies, wherein we developed post mortem CT imagery analysis, proved to be yet another valuable contribution to the field. The CT imaging technology allowed us to preserve the specimen while simultaneously conducting diagnostic studies. This innovative technique resulted in my first published paper, but because I did not have a "PhD" following my name, Dr. Hunt had to present the paper and participate in the international conference. Nevertheless, I was honored to know that my work had been recognized by the scientific community.

The first time I saw the mummies on display in the Museum of Natural History at the Smithsonian, I was taken aback. My dancing skeleton dream had materialized before me. There were four mummies on display. This validated something for me. Although I don't believe in the supernatural, I feel that our science has not tapped into all of its available knowledge. We are given more glimpses through our subconscious mind.

More and more prominent symbols appeared in my dreams and nightmares. They were more real to me than ever before because of the validation the mummies on display provided. The meaning of many of my dreams, past and present, still remained unknown, but a large part of me believed that their answers would be revealed later in my life.

I also worked with forensic anthropologists and the FBI on landmark homicide cases involving serial murders. Dr. Hunt had phoned me during work hours at the hospital to ask if I might look over one of his latest cases. He explained that there was very little bone to work with and that the investigators were worried that they might destroy the evidence by using conventional techniques to acquire a DNA strain from weather-exposed bone. I was happy to help him.

Dr. Hunt arrived at my door around 3:00 p.m. that same day.

"What do you have for me, Dr. Dave?" I asked.

"Well, I have a little baggy with some bone and bone fragments," he responded. "Can you do something with them to help us determine to whom they belong?"

He handed me the baggy that contained a portion of a jaw, a couple of teeth, and portion of cervical spine. I pondered for a minute before probing, "I have an X but I need a Y. Do you have any images or X-rays, even a body on potentials?"

"I can get them," he assured me.

"So have you guys done carbon dating yet?"

"Well, that's the problem. We can't do CD because it will destroy the evidence. Because of how the bones were found, it would be too risky a test to run. We wouldn't want to lose this evidence."

"Is this an important case? "I raised an eyebrow." How did they find the bones?"

"Well, if I tell ya, I'd have to kill ya."

"Oh." It tensed a little, "I guess mum's the word on this one."

"It's a Fed case," he then explained.

A few hours later, I received stacks of X-rays of potential victims. These were of bones the FBI believed were possibilities in Dr. Hunt's baggy. Dave explained that without a possible match, the evidence could not be used to make a conviction.

It had become common for researchers, federal agencies, and department heads to request my help on forensic cases. The challenge with this particular case was the time constraint. The court date was in four days. That gave us three days to develop an innovative technique to identify the victim correctly, and to outline the scientific process by which we came up with the evidence to be presented to the jury.

I opened the baggy and removed the evidence. I placed the single cervical vertebra, several teeth, and a small part of a mandible before me. The bones were weathered, dry, and discolored. I reflected once again on my dancing skeletons dream. I remembered the latter part of the dream, the solitary skull lying on the floor in the back of the house. The prominent jaw and teeth in my dream were not unlike the evidence lying before me now. Another premonition? But why… why me? It was a peculiar sort of déjà vu, the kind I was growing accustomed to by then. In a sense, I was comforted, as if some higher power was letting me know I was on the right path.

It took seventeen hours of work before I came up with a technique that was for the first time replicable and therefore could be tested again with other specimens. The job was completed and the evidence was successfully used in court. I didn't receive any details about the trial until years later. When I found out whose trial I'd slaved over, if only for three days, I was in a state of shock. The fragments of bone were evidence for the Jeffrey Dahmer serial murder trials. My work had been used to help determine the identity of the first victim Dahmer had brutally murdered and dismembered. Dahmer had smashed the bones into tiny pieces near a creek on his family's property. The bones were discovered after he gleefully described in detail how he had murdered and disposed of each one of his victims.

The experience of learning from Dr. Hunt and other masters in my field of study made my budding career in forensics nothing short of extraordinary. Not only did my knowledge of disease, pathology, physiology and forensics expand, but I also discovered how these factors are intricately linked to history, cultural diversity, philosophy, and religion around the world.

Working in forensics also brought me face to face with the reality of death, a constant reminder of life's frailty. After all, the cadavers I'd been working with were once living, breathing human beings long before I came to know them as inanimate corpses. Knowledge is worth nothing if not applied. The knowledge I gained from working with these lifeless beings was invaluable. In some cases, I was able to uncover clues to human existence from thousands of years past, while in others, my research gave closure to those who had lost loved ones suddenly and traumatically. Each new discovery both fascinated and humbled me and my time at George Washington University Medical Center passed quickly.

Eventually, I moved out of my condominium and bought a 1930's brick colonial house in a wonderful, historic part of Silver Spring, Maryland. The streets were lined with large oaks and friendly neighbors. I spent a small fortune and much of my free time renovating this house, which I loved. There was nothing better than lounging in front of the old fireplace in the living room with a good book and my cat, Carly.

Although I had settled into my home and my routine, my schedule was still hectic. My days managing the radiology department's five divisions and 150 employees began at 6:00 a.m. When I wasn't at the hospital, I was on 24-hour on-call duty; I was traveling, consulting, and overseeing the five research grants I had procured, not to mention taking evening classes at the University. I relished what little downtime I was able to fit in.

As I lay down to sleep the dream of the mummies came to the forefront of my mind. Was the dream of the farm skeletons for telling, what was to be or something else? Is there a correlation of symbols with reality or did I just make it all up? With only a few dreams to go on, I was reluctant to think that there was some unusual activity with my mind but as I woke, strange things began to happen.

CHAPTER SEVEN

A Different Kind of Dream

On an ordinary winter evening after work, traversing the chilly streets of D.C. to my car, I envisioned a hot bath after another strenuous day at work. Driving home in the midst of rush hour was actually something I enjoyed because it forced me to finally slow down and reflect on my day. It was around 8:30 p.m.; the city lights glistened off of the wet streets as the crisp night air continued to cool. Silhouettes of leafless trees lined 16th Street, and as I headed home toward the Maryland beltway, it began to snow.

After a soak in the tub, I spent the evening warming myself by the fire with my cat Carly while running numbers through my head for a physics exam the following evening. Exhausted, I sank into bed before midnight and drifted off to sleep. Sometime before dawn, a vivid dream and the startling sound of a honking horn somewhere along my street broke my sleep. I glanced out the window, and then at the clock, it was only 4:30a.m.! Feeling cheated, I tried to fall back asleep, but the dream consumed me. The image was incredibly clear but its meaning escaped me.

I am dressed in shorts and a t-shirt, standing in front of an airplane in the desert. The haze is just burning off in the morning sun, and I see the outline of mountains along the horizon. The airplane has "World Care" written on its side. I'm holding a clipboard and checking what seems to be a large load of shipping boxes spread out before me on the sandy airstrip.

Realizing that sleep was no longer an option, while in the wake of a dream, I recorded that lucid image with a picture in my journal before preparing for another day at work. That afternoon at the hospital, I had a chat with Dr. Valentine, a colleague and psychologist with a special interest in dream interpretations and the teachings of Carl Jung. Dr. Valentine's responses to my inquiries were kind and non-threatening. He assured me that I was not losing my mind, but didn't give me the answers I was looking for.

"It sounds to me like you live a very busy life," he said with a grin. "I'd like to hear more about your dreams. I want you to know that there is nothing to be afraid of. Most people sleep and dream for a third of their lives."

I blurted out, "My dreams are beginning to freak me out. They've been pretty strange for a while now actually. Sure, everybody dreams, but is it normal to have predictive dreams? And is it normal for these predictive dreams to really come true?" There it was.

"Let me think about this for a while," he responded after a long pause. "I'll call you to set up a time to discuss your dreams in greater detail. In the meantime, don't be afraid. Your dreams are healthy – they are telling you something. I'd be interested to see your dream journals when we get together again. We can talk them through."

As I left, I felt as though he had tricked me into having

a therapy session. I resolved to forget about it at happy hour. Once there though, my friend Carol convinced me that I needed to meet with Dr. Valentine next week after all. Maybe it was just because she and every other woman had the hots for him (a la *McDreamy*). I jokingly told her that she had been working in pediatrics far too long, while she tried to convince me that my dreams were the result of some repressed issues from my childhood, surfacing via my subconscious. I assured her that was *not* the case. However, she made a good argument that perhaps I needed to decompress from being overworked and therefore it would be worthwhile it to speak with Dr. Valentine, if only to quiet my mind.

So, once again I found myself faced with Dr. Valentine. I was a little worried about what he might say to our colleagues if I divulged all of my crazy dreams, so I kept my guard up. Being labeled a lunatic would have been pretty devastating to my career. What am I doing here, I wondered, as the questions began. But it was too late to turn around and leave.

Recognizing my discomfort, he said, "Lisa, we're colleagues. Call me Brad."

"Thanks, Brad," I responded with a smirk.

"Lisa, whatever we talk about here is confidential."

God, could this guy read my mind?

He continued, "I've been doing dream work for years, and I find it to be a truly fascinating and intricate part of our human consciousness. So tell me about yourself. Where did you grow up? Where is your family?" His voice was comforting.

He sat back and relaxed and I began to feel more comfortable. I told him about my dreams and the way they came true at later points in my life. I told him how some of the dreams had questions still unanswered, and how sometimes in my waking life, I wonder about the meanings of my dreams. We looked through my journal and he asked me some questions. He had no groundbreaking insights into my dream life, but he validated my dreams in a way that allowed me to move forward and accept them as a normal, functioning part of my life.

Habitually, every evening before bed, I stepped outside onto my porch, looked up at the moon and stars and said, "Hello," to the universe and thanked God for another good day. I didn't know that at the time I was nearing the edge of the comfortable plateau I'd come to know for the past few years. Financial and emotional stability were things I was beginning to take for granted. My graduation from George Washington was fast approaching, and with it came news that the hospital was being sold off, so my position would soon be eliminated. Rather than requesting my resignation, according to a memorandum sent to me and God knows how many others, the hospital administration explained only that changes were being made and it would be in my best interest to start looking for another position elsewhere.

Around the same time in early 1994, Betty, a friend from the radiologist group in Washington called me with horrible news about her 27 year old daughter, Pamela, who had been killed when she was pushed out of a speeding car on I-95 in Maryland. I realized that a dream of mine from several years earlier had foretold this awful event.

Betty and I had worked together in the past, but I'd never met her daughter Pamela, though I supposed Betty must have mentioned her.

That night I took out my journal and discovered this dream had come to me early in June, 1985:

I'm driving through a powerful, raging storm with my sisters, Stephanie and Cathy, my friend, Betty, and her daughter, Pamela.

The next thing I know, I'm in a sailboat with Betty, as Pamela sits in a car near the dock. She's looking at a detailed road map. Betty and I sail to the edge of the storm, leaving Pamela behind. I warn Betty that we should go back because the storm is dangerous. When we return to the calm water, the car is still next to the dock, but Pamela is standing at a far distance away, along the highway. The Map, which is now lying on the dock, reveals our location...we are on the I-95, in Maryland

This shook me tremendously. I had no interest in having some freak ability to foresee tragedies. I didn't understand why I had been given this information years earlier. Worst of all, I felt afraid to talk about it. As I continued recording subsequent dreams, I worried about what I was putting down in writing.

I didn't want to be stigmatized by people connecting me with being a psychic, but after fifteen years of experiencing dream visions, it was time to find out what was happening to me. I had already surrendered to the fact that my prophetic dreams were an integral part of my life; the next step, I decided, was to enlist a doctor friend, Dellie, to help me interpret my dream journals dating back to 1979.

In our interpretations, we found patterns of symbols I could relate to personally, as well as universal symbols of world events over which I had no control. We noticed that many of my dreams preceded events that happened two or three years later.

Ultimately, Dellie suggested that I visit a dream consultant that she knew. Neither Dellie nor I gave the consultant any personal information about me, not even as much as my name. The consultant worked from her home in rural Maryland. The warm summer breeze blew through my open window and put me at ease as we drove toward the consultation. As I turned off the main street onto a dirt road toward the consultant's quaint farmhouse, the quiet, breezy moment was abruptly interrupted by a flock of chickens darting past my car. The wind animated the flags and pinwheel lawn ornaments along the walkway to a welcoming pink front door.

A mystical-looking woman with long white hair and crystal blue eyes greeted us at the door. She was dressed in a purple and pink robe. She led me upstairs to a room where she conducted her sessions. When I gave her a fake name, she told me it wasn't necessary to give her a name at all. A wave of relief rushed through me. We sat down comfortably on piles of plump pillows that formed a seating area on the floor.

She told me that my energy was strong, but that I was resisting what was going on around me. She saw a lot of travel in my future. When she said I was a teacher, my internal reaction was that I had no interest at all in being a teacher. Was this for real?

Then she said, "This is all I will tell you. You have the gift. You will be given more information when you need it."

She ended the session abruptly, giving me back my money and adding, "Don't waste your money seeing more people like me. Your path is already set and you will do great things."

More than a little confused, I thanked her for her insights and accepted the returned money. After hearing this information that was too vague to be useful, I immediately dismissed her prediction. Little did I know how her insight would begin to materialize.

CHAPTER EIGHT

Opening my Heart

Although the hospital was up for sale, it was still business as usual for now, and my department was running smoothly. I considered sending out applications for other positions in order to have something lined up when the hospital finally sold. But I decided to put the job search on hold for the time being and resolved to take a long overdue vacation instead.

I hadn't taken a break in years, so after making sure that I had enough time off, and that my department in the hospital would be covered during my absence, I booked a trip to Mexico with a friend. It was cold in D.C., and I needed to get away. A week at the beach in Puerto Vallarta sounded like just what I needed.

My previous travels with the military opened up my curiosity to seek out life beyond tourist traps, and Puerto Vallarta was no exception. I wanted to visit the countryside, away from the fancy area that catered to well-heeled gringos. Far from the beach, the view inland revealed beautiful and lush landscapes, and I was curious to find out about the people who lived there. I recalled some of the Mexican immigrants who used to stay at my grandmother's boarding house, and wondered why anybody would want to leave a place that looked so lovely and green for the harsh, urban sprawl of south Chicago.

Where we stayed was beautiful and luxurious amenities abounded in the hotel in Puerto Vallarta. I gazed out over the patio to admire the calm, inviting ocean. After we rested for a while, my friend and I decided to go for a walk. As we made our way down the manicured streets, I pulled her off of the main corridor. We walked away from the mainstream American stores and fast food chains, the parts we were supposed to see, the parts that were tourist approved. Within two blocks, we found shacks built from pallets and crates, clothing hanging from twisted vines to dry, and chickens running wildly, free from their coops. Along our real world tour, there was a community water area where women washed clothes, and a creek nearby where children bathed.

There were literally hundreds of shack-like homes that appeared identical to one another, most without electricity. As we wandered through residential areas that opened up into marketplaces at every block or so, new faces greeted us and forged permanent pictures in my memory. In the distance, a man with a donkey cart slowly made his way to the local market area we'd stumbled upon.

A young woman, weathered by the sun, sold fresh fruit outside of her house, while another cooked fresh tortillas, calling out to her four children playing in the dirt road.

As my friend and I continued to walk farther into the village, we saw a woman sitting beside her child, a little girl wrapped in a blanket and sleeping peacefully inside of a cardboard box. Hours passed as we continued to meander through the village.

My friend and I eventually found our way back to the manufactured noises and bustle of the touristy main drag and headed back to our hotel. We were both at a loss for words over what we'd witnessed and the contrast to our resort area. We grabbed towels and headed to the beach in contemplative silence.

Sitting on the beach, looking out across the vast ocean, I thought about my childhood in Chicago in relation to what I had just seen. I was reminded that people everywhere struggle with poverty.

For the rest of our trip in Mexico, we spent more time wandering through the back roads of the countryside and found a sense of peace and belonging as we walked amongst the people of that region. I wondered how they came to be so impoverished, and if they yearned for change like many of the workers who had stayed at my grandmother's boardinghouse.

On our return to the airport, driving past those same impoverished areas, the taxi driver made a snide comment, referring to the people in the streets as pests while gesturing with his hands and muttering something that sounded profane in Spanish.

Back home in D.C., I kept envisioning the people and poverty of Puerto Vallarta. They lived with no running water, in houses built of flimsy pallets, with provisions collected from the local dump. I couldn't get the image of the little girl in the cardboard box out of my mind. I kept contrasting...

I was also reminded that the people struggling with poverty in Mexico were not alone. Every day, I encountered poor people living right there in D.C., the capital city of our great country, the land of opportunity. Homeless people slept alone on cold sidewalks while people in suits trekked pass them on their way to fancy jobs, blind to the poverty at their doorsteps.

Sullenly I returned to work with the knowledge that I would soon be losing my job once the hospital was sold. I had worked so hard and come so far in my career to be dropped like this. Then again, this decision was far bigger than me and my job at the hospital. I always believed that if I worked hard enough and sacrificed for what I believed in, then the universe would be good to me. I had to stay positive that everything would align in the end, that maybe there was a reason for this upheaval at work.

During a break from work one snowy night, I was carrying leftover Chinese food back to the hospital when I came across a homeless man curled up on a bench, wearing only one small shoe with the toes cut out. A bag of garbage served as his pillow and his belongings were packed neatly beside him in a shopping cart. He wore layers of dirty clothing but not enough to protect him from the winter cold. As I placed my leftover food beside him on the bench, I worried that he might get frostbite.

Later that night, the same homeless man came to the front desk of the hospital. For hours, he was shuffled around from wheelchair to stretcher and back to wheelchair again, as stretchers were needed for higher priority patients. A nurse wrapped the poor man in blankets, but it appeared that gangrene may have already set into his toes.

One of the ER doctors looked at the man's toes and recommended an X-ray. I sent him to radiology for some tests, which required him to remove his clothing and his shoe. The smell of rotten flesh and stale alcohol permeated the room. The doctor wanted to admit him but the man refused. With little else to do we found some new garments and shoes for him to wear when he was ready to leave. This gesture of humanity was done out of a common, unspoken understanding. We helped someone in this way almost every night.

My interactions with the poor, sick, and needy, helped transform my view of the world. I was becoming more emotionally sensitive to the people around me without even knowing them. I had a lot of empathy for people who struggled in life, especially with poverty and illness.

Once, on the way into the radiology room with an older African-American gentleman who was very ill, I felt compelled to hold his hand. I held his hand tight and looked into his eyes, and something told me he was going to die. It was an incredibly intimate moment, as if time stopped around me. I continued looking into his big, brown eyes, wanting to give him a sense of peace, and I told him that it was okay to go. He looked at me knowingly, through tears, as if he had resigned to his fate. Moments later, he died.

I finally graduated from college in May 1994, while still working at GWUMC, and still uncertain about my future employment. It was a perfect spring day, with just a few cirrus clouds floating across a true blue sky on a gentle breeze coming off the Potomac. Hillary Clinton was our keynote speaker, an icon of female power, strength, and courage. The ceremony overlooked the White House and the beautifully manicured lawns surrounding the monuments of our great forefathers. I reminded myself, today is a good day. I proudly sat in the front row surrounded by the graduating class. My mom, step-dad, sister, niece, and nephew had made the trip all the way from Illinois to watch me graduate. I was the first person in my family to graduate from college, so it was a big day for everyone.

Hillary Clinton's words reminded me of just how much I had accomplished so far in my lifetime. Most importantly, in graduating from college, I'd completed a goal I had been working toward for fourteen years. I was struck by Hillary's poise, confidence, and determination in telling my classmates and me that we are the future, and the future looks great. As roll began to be called, and students stepped one by one onto the stage, I began to cry. It was more than a sentimental moment. It hit me then that each of us has a story to tell. We are all filled with endless potential. When it was my turn to walk on stage and accept my diploma, shake the dean's hand and walk back to my chair, my life had changed forever. I had acquired my college diploma; the world was my oyster. We all threw our caps into the air and I looked back at my Mom, with tears flowing down my face. She smiled, waved to me, and never looked so proud.

The next month, as I sat in my office at the hospital reviewing radiology schedules, an older colleague appeared at my door.

"Hello, Dr. James," I smiled cordially, "how are you doing this fine day?"

"Fine, Lisa, well indeed. I wonder if you can help me?" His soft, southern accent made it impossible to be frustrated by the interruption.

I readjusted my glasses as he continued, "Have you ever traveled to Mexico or South America?" I decided to tell him about a trip I took while in the Army - long before Puerto Vallarta. "Well I drove to Mexico with a friend from the military. It opened my eyes to impoverished conditions across the border. "

"How did you get in?"

"My military I.D. allowed me to traverse the border to visit my friend Maria's small town just west of Laredo, Texas, in the Tamaulipas province."

He paused for a moment then grabbed a chair and sat next to me. I wasn't sure where the conversation was going, and then he let loose with a large hum. "So what was your experience?"

"Well, we crossed the Rio Grande and turned off the main road and down a dusty pitted street. "

"No, I mean what did you see and what was your experience?"

OK...I closed my eyes, as my mind began to replay the experience I began to talk.

"I remember as we drove down the streets, I became transfixed by a woman hanging clothes on a line outside of a wooden shack as we approached. I asked Maria, 'Is that your house?'

'Yes, this is where I grew up,' she replied. We were delivering some medical supplies to a small village consisting of shacks like this one, scarcely shaded trees, and a stream that was nearly dry. As we drove through the village, Maria recounted her story of sexual abuse as a child that led to being removed from the village and sent to the United States. Her uncle's abuse resulted in a teen pregnancy. She was sent across the border with a female relative and was taken to a back alley doctor for an abortion. After almost bleeding to death, she wound up in a halfway house to recover. She found work as a maid to pay for the abortion.

"At eighteen, Maria moved to San Antonio where she enrolled in school, and vowed never to return to that life again. Maria always dreamed of becoming a nurse. She shared her desire to help keep young teenage girls from having the same bad experience that she had. She wanted to educate young girls about sexual abuse.

"We were silent for the next couple of miles, both observing the community around us. At our stop, children covered in dirt with no shirts or shoes, ran to the car begging us for anything we had, their hands outstretched to us, their eyebrows raised in hope and expectation. Maria's story left me to wonder how many of these children in her village had also been abused. How many of them had any hope for their future?"

I became silent and recalled my own childhood in Harvey, Illinois. It seemed charmed by comparison. Our standard of growing up poor was very different from the poverty of this small village. I had a safe home, after all. I had options for living my life, whereas these children had no choice. Maria getting out was an exception. These children were stuck, I realized. Living without options, without freedom of choice...privileges I took for granted for so long. This trip to Mexico lasted only about ten hours or so, but the impression it made on me lasted a lifetime.

Dr. Everett grabbed his chin and began to get up. "Good, good. I've recently returned from Venezuela where one of the attending physicians asked me if I might know of a consultant capable of a needs assessment and feasibility study for hospital and clinical use in Caracas."

I nodded, allowing him to continue once more.

"Actually, it's my son's company and he's just starting off. I spoke with your director and he recommended you."

"Why me?" I wondered aloud, "I don't mind helping you, sir, but I've only done needs assessments for the departments here, and..."

"Well," he interrupted, "Your director is the best in his field, and I respect his recommendation. He told me about your military experience and about the great work you've done for his department over the past four years. That's not all. He went on about your attention to detail, problem solving and technical skills, and believed that all of these attributes make you the ideal candidate for this job."

"Wow"... I was flattered.

"So what do you think?" He wanted an answer. I merely nodded, already enticed by the opportunities awaiting me in Venezuela.

He continued, "So I want you to meet my son tonight after work. His name is Everett James III, and he's a lawyer. There's a great little restaurant around the corner on K Street. He'll give you the details there. I just know it will be a great experience for you. And if that's not enough, your director has already approved covering your time on the trip since it is job-related. You will need a passport if you don't have one and we will take care of the rest. See you at seven tonight?"

"Yes sir! See you then." I loved a challenge and this was an opportunity to connect with the world outside of the hospital.

I met Everett for dinner later that night. He was young, kind, tall, handsome, and eager to make his project work. His goal was to confirm the need for radiology equipment and other supplies in Venezuelan facilities so that he could obtain funding for infrastructure from the World Bank. As soon as I returned home that evening, I searched through everything I could find about Venezuela to find out what I had gotten myself into. I had already said yes out of impulse, though I felt like saying no wasn't an option for me anyhow. The trip was scheduled for December, only a few months away!

In the meantime, I started to send out resumes. I felt that I had already accomplished what I had set out to do for the department, and that it was time to move on. I had my degree and legitimate experience. With these credentials, it would be easy to find a new position, right? Wrong!

Healthcare was changing rapidly. Despite what individuals

were able to do, high-end corporate decisions were dictating the destiny of the new medical age of the emerging HMO. No longer could doctors just be doctors. Insurance companies were gearing up to make life hell for the medical professionals and for the patients. I knew that changes were coming, and I had to be ready for changes within my field.

Two applications seemed like good odds. I applied for a directorship of radiology at the University of Kentucky. Then I saw an advertisement in a trade magazine for an associate director of radiology at University Medical Center in Tucson, Arizona, so I sent out another resume. A couple months later I was invited to Tucson for an interview. I flew out to Arizona and interviewed on my birthday, August 29th, 1994.

When I arrived in Tucson it was as if hell had come to the earth, it was so damn hot. It reminded me of my military training in the middle of July in Alabama, but it was the worst of the season so I perspired and persevered. I felt optimistic about my future as I interviewed with the entire department of over 160 employees and a multitude of administrators.

Two days after my return to Washington D.C., the director from University Medical Center in Tucson called to offer me the position! I graciously accepted. I was very sad to leave my crew at the hospital in D.C. I had a great boss who believed in me and granted me creative space and autonomy. It was unfortunate that the hospital was being sold, as the team I was working with had become a second family. I turned in my resignation and said my goodbyes, thankful for all that I had learned and for the relationships built.

During the fifteen years that I lived in Washington, D.C., I had created a lot of artwork. As parting gifts, I gave my friends my pictures and paintings as appreciation for their friendship over the years. There was a lot of crying, laughing and partying. An era of wonderful growth and experience was coming to a close. I always say that I cut my teeth at GWUMC. The knowledge and experience I gained while working there was the foundation for what I'd soon build in the future of my medical career. Little did I know what lie ahead.

CHAPTER NINE

A Move to the Desert

The sadness I felt about leaving Washington, D.C. was quieted by the impending move to Tucson, Arizona. What would the desert hold for me, I wondered. Freezing winters no more, I thought. Also, I had a cousin, Elaine, who lived in Tucson, which would make the transition into a new place easier. I phoned her a few weeks before I was set to move and she generously offered to let me stay with her until I found a place of my own.

As for getting my possessions to Tucson, that proved to be a bit tougher. I had to plan how I was going to travel there. I was cautiously optimistic as I called my father, having been estranged from him for the past several years. I asked him for his help in making the move, a 2,700 mile drive across the country. I thought that some one-on-one time might help to repair old wounds. It was a once in a lifetime opportunity to confront him about issues that I needed closure on. In a way, it was a second chance to heal our relationship, and deep down I feared that it was our last chance. He quickly agreed, although I wasn't sure if he realized exactly what he was getting himself into, but Dad was happy to be on a road trip, back in his element again.

After being practically silent in the car for a day and a half, Dad finally said, "Hey, Lis, you know why I travel and move around so much? So that God can never find me."

I thought about that for a while, then replied, "You know, I think God can find you moving or not. You're just lucky he's busy on another highway."

We both sat silent as we traveled until the weather changed, so we had something benign to talk about. The one thing I always enjoyed was my Dad's sense of humor and his ability to laugh at life's misfortunes. Even though the trip was long and awkward at times, it brought on a sense of peace between my father and me, something we'd both wanted without saying so for years. It's funny, no matter how old children grow; they still desire their parents' love and affection more than anything. I was happy to know that even if my father wasn't entertained by me as a child, at least he was learning to love me as an adult.

We flowed into hot, sweaty Tucson, cat and all, like warm honey. I stayed for a while with my cousin before buying a small house in Oro Valley outside of the city, with beautiful views of the Santa Catalina Mountains. The home was peaceful, and just the right size to easily maintain. I joined a professional women's golf league that met every Thursday for nine holes after work. Life was good.

After working in D.C., in an inner-city hospital contaminated with personnel problems and nearby drug rings, scandals, rapes, murders, and thieves, the new job at University of Arizona Medical Center was a breeze. The problems I encountered in Tucson seemed to be a lot less severe, and more personal in nature. The hospital suffered mostly from petty egos and small town politics. It was like there was nothing better to do than pry and gossip. Their problems were the problems of the privileged. For example, an employee once asked me for a raise because she had just bought a new car. Well, in that case…

Another employee told me she could not come to work because she had to watch the final episode of *All My Children*. Although I found myself irritated at times by these trivial matters, I had to keep a sense of humor about these insignificant annoyances. Most times, it seemed as if there wasn't a problem the hospital could throw at me that I couldn't solve.

I still had two unfinished research projects from Washington D.C. to complete for Dr. Everett James, with trips to Mexico, Guatemala, and Venezuela scheduled before the end of the year. I was burning the candle at both ends. The desert climate of Tucson was harsh and my body was still adjusting to the dryness and heat. I assumed that feeling tired and rundown was normal. My medical insurance would not kick in until after my probation period was over, so I opted not to go to the doctor.

Then I received a disturbing call from my sister, Cathy. Apparently, upon returning home from helping me move to Tucson, my father had developed an unknown respiratory ailment that would not go away. Had our trip really been a last chance opportunity? I was so grateful for it then. The doctors were still conducting tests on my father, I was still feeling under the weather, and I noticed my cat Carly was also losing weight. My father was put on some medication, my cat Carly died, and I continued to wait for health insurance. It was tough losing Carly, but I was thankful that my father would be well again soon. Were our sudden illnesses all related? I had to assume so for now.

I was scheduled to go to Guatemala to do a medical assessment in November. My friend Denise, whom I'd met on my flight from Dallas to D.C., was now living in Guatemala as a Peace Corps volunteer. I contacted her to see if she could assist me with translations while I did my evaluations. She agreed, and I was looking forward to having the opportunity to meet with her again.

One day before I was scheduled to leave, I broke out in an awful fever. Just my luck, I thought. The doctors at University Medical Center urged me to get a chest X-ray, and I agreed. Later that day, the radiologist showed me my X-ray, which displayed a large white mass in the upper left lobe of my lungs. The doctors requested a biopsy, but I impatiently refused. I had a flight to catch in ten hours! I asked the radiologist what he thought it was, explaining that my fever had come on suddenly, only over the past two days.

"You have Valley Fever pneumonia, indigenous to the Southwest, "he explained." You can't take anything for it. It will run its course and you'll do okay. You're new to these parts, so you've been exposed. It's not contagious. You can travel, but your immune system is compromised, so avoid exposure to other diseases."

Great! Thanks Doc.

I trusted him. He had been reading chest X-rays for forty years, so I figured he recognized my symptoms. The doctors recommended that I postpone the trip to get some rest, but canceling my trip to Guatemala was in my book, not an option. After all, I felt only slightly run down, a little tired, with minor chest pain. It was manageable. I gave some blood for testing, and told them I'd be back in six days, hopefully feeling sufficiently recovered.

I called my father that evening and told him to go down to the Veteran's Hospital and get a chest X-ray. I figured that it was likely that he was suffering from the same malady as my cat and I.

And so, medication in hand and still a bit drowsy, my unforgettable, life-altering trip to Guatemala began. Antigua's lush green foliage was welcoming compared to the brown desert of Arizona. It was fall, and cool breezes cut through meandering cobblestone streets as lights went dim. Life seemed simple yet difficult. My hotel accommodations were basic – a bed, a cold-water shower, and a small sink. My friend Denise had a flat around the corner that could sleep only one. Exhausted from my trip, I settled in, showered, and quickly fell asleep.

Early the next morning I awoke to find a basket on my doorstep, spilling over with wonderful fresh fruit, baked breads, and cheeses. What a warm welcome I thought. I began my day with a skip in my step (and some delicious food in my belly), as I set out to explore the city.

As I wandered through the village, the poverty and rawness quickly became apparent. Children slept in boxes on the street beside their parents, who were kneading bread and selling fresh fruit to earn a living. Uneven slabs of poured concrete sidewalks lined streets made of dirt and stone. I had to watch out for cars speeding dangerously down the narrow roads. At dusk, Denise and I walked quickly and closely together to avoid the many pickpockets lurking on the streets. To conserve energy, the government turned off the electricity periodically, for a minimum of eight hours per day. Residents depended on fireplaces for hot water, and ate mostly raw food throughout the day.

Denise and I began our day by visiting the clinic and local humanitarian aid stations around the community. I quickly realized that the medical supplies and health aids the clinic had requested were mere band-aids to cover up the community's problems. Although my knowledge of Guatemala's political situation was limited, I sensed that this band-aid philosophy was part of the problem.

The more I wandered around small villages, the more the widespread poverty and pain consumed me. I felt compelled not only to help, but to make a lasting change. I saw children and

71

adults standing outside of the fence of a dilapidated school while visiting the mountain villages of Panachele. When asked why they were not in school, a man replied in broken English that the children couldn't attend because their families could not pay for school supplies. Instinctively, I handed out the pencils and notebook paper I carried with me to the children. They were eager and grateful to receive them. It struck me how something as simple as a pencil and piece of paper could have such an impact on these children. My heart shuddered. I was filled with a painful yearning to understand why these people were so impoverished, and I wanted desperately to ease them out of their struggle with basic needs that included education.

That night, I had the same dream that I'd had earlier that year, before I moved to Tucson.

I am dressed in shorts and a t-shirt, standing in front of an airplane in the desert where the haze is just burning off in the morning sun. The airplane has "World Care" written on its side. I'm holding a clipboard and checking what seems to be a large load of shipping boxes spread before me on the sandy airstrip.

I awoke in a pool of sweat with a 103-degree fever. I could barely take in a breath and I had a terrible pain in my chest. Denise helped get me to the doctor at the only clinic in town. The doctor concluded that it was pneumonia, gave me antibiotics, and ordered me to stay in bed. But I only had two more days remaining on my trip, and I was determined to make the most of my time.

Although I went to Guatemala to investigate health conditions, I realized that what the people really needed were more basic education resources. Relative to the average income of the people living in Guatemala, school supplies were extremely expensive. Healthcare supplies were temporary and scarce, an issue that could be linked back to the lack of available resources for basic education. The inadequate healthcare system or lack thereof was linked more to inadequate education than to the lack of equipment. Knowledge needed to come first, this much I knew. Without education, the Guatemalan people seemed merely to exist, continuing to populate, only to be controlled and manipulated by politics for money and power.   Mortality rates were high; people died young because there was no way for them to improve their condition.   This scenario had repeated itself historically throughout world, and was continuing to do so in modern times.

The night before I left for the US, Denise and I dined at a local restaurant that served fresh fruit and fish. Everything was doused in lime, a fruit that grew everywhere in Antigua. After dinner, we attended a performance in which actors in traditional Guatemalan dress--large masks and headdresses--danced on a stone stage in an outdoor, torch-lit theater. Locals sold nuts and juices outside the venue.

I returned home to Tucson. The doctor informed me that I had both Valley Fever and Hepatitis. Although I was aware of the risk of traveling to Guatemala against the advice of the doctor, the trip was a necessary and pivotal experience for me. Hepatitis was worth it and curable, besides. I was grateful that I had the option and ability to obtain modern medicine, an impossible luxury to the villagers in Guatemala and many around the world. How is it that we have so much and they have so little?

CHAPTER TEN

Epiphany

As I recovered from my illness, my mind transfixed on the Guatemalan children I'd met who couldn't afford to go to school. My experience there left me with a new awareness of the world around me. I promised myself to take school supplies with me on all future trips to developing countries.

I began collecting school supplies by asking colleagues to clean out their drawers at the office. Some items were new and some were used; anything would do. In my office alone, we accumulated enough supplies for 23 children. When I returned to Guatemala the following year (for the record, in *excellent* health), I distributed the supplies to the children hanging around the schoolyard as I had the year before. They were so grateful for the pencils and paper. Some of the children gathered in a circle and pretended that they were in a classroom. One child became the teacher and the other children sat obediently, waiting for instruction. The pain I'd felt the year before was replaced with a good feeling that I was making a positive contribution to the lives of these children.

Back in Radiology at UMC in Tucson, the hospital's history of financial problems began to unravel before my eyes. I reviewed and cleaned up the billing system, a task that had not been addressed for several years. The defunct system in existence at that time was the cause of much of the financial loss. Radiology was one the largest and most lucrative departments in the hospital, and had to carry the financial weight of other departments that were not as successful. Efficient operation was critical.

The technical side of radiology made it difficult to make sound personnel and financial decisions without running the risk of simultaneously compromising patient care. I brought this area of expertise to the department from my job and experiences in DC. I was able to improve the functioning of the department with limited resources. My staff was invaluable in this process. They were the machines with heart that provided unprecedented patient care. I was contributing to the improvement of patient care by focusing on the management and technical staff's morale.

Healthcare was becoming an increasingly challenging field because of more and more regulations, limited resources, and the devaluation of technical knowledge. The administration rated job performance according to how cut-throat a worker could be, and how many people could be eliminated of in order to save the hospital money. Even though my department brought in huge revenues it wasn't enough to offset other departments' losses. Cash flow was the bottom line. No one was left unaffected by downsizing, restructuring, and the reorganizing of the practice of medicine. As a result, both doctor and patient suffered the wrath while many administrators dove into cutting personnel from the start. I felt there were other methods that could be adjusted to makeup of the staff which I began to demonstrate.

By day I worked in the hospital, while at night I focused

on international programs and school supply collections for children. A month after I returned from Guatemala, I headed to Venezuela where I began to work with Dr. Everett James. Although I was working full time at UMC, I fulfilled my prior consulting commitment to Everett, who was in charge of negotiating between the World Bank and the Venezuelan government, regarding healthcare funding. My job was to assess the country's need for health facilities and supplies, and to provide a report to support the government's request to the World Bank for millions of dollars of funding. Specifically, the Venezuelan Ministry of Health needed to justify a very expensive piece of medical equipment in one of their hospitals in order to be granted the requested funds.

We toured fifteen hospitals and met with high officials and dignitaries. General health in the capital city, Caracas, was appalling. It was obvious that even the most basic needs were not met. Beams protruded from ceilings. Hospitals had no windows and no ventilation. Women gave birth in hallways. Patients lay on tables and dilapidated stretchers covered in yellow-stained linens. There were no sterile procedures to be found. Doctors reused gloves on the operating table, overlapping three sets at a time to ensure that there were no holes. Even in the more sterile environments, where I wore a mask and surgical gown, I was taken aback by the lack of hygienic procedures and rooms. The floors had open drains, out of which roaches and water bugs crept.

The entire experience infuriated me. How could the Venezuelan government have the audacity to request expensive MRI equipment when what they really needed was a lesson in hygiene, illness, and a few doctors who actually gave a damn about helping others, not simply making do?

I photographed what I saw, throughout the villages,

outside of the schoolyard, and in make-shift clinics. I brought the pictures along to the meeting with the Minister of Health, which took place at his lush palace. When we arrived at the estate, we were greeted by servants and escorted through lavishly furnished rooms, in stark contrast to the devastating poverty suffered by most of the population outside of the Minister's mansion.

The Minister of Health was eager to receive a positive report from me so that it could be forwarded to the World Bank. He was cordial and personal with me but I had no intention of granting him the report. Was he oblivious to the world outside of his door, or simply in denial? He seemed to care only about obtaining funding, with no intention of applying those funds where they were truly needed - in education, in primary school, and primary care. Despite the hospital's need for money to improve their conditions, I simply couldn't write out a report to fund a major piece of medical equipment. I felt strongly that this was not where the money should be allocated. Avoiding confrontation, I remained quiet about the details of the report. It crossed my mind that it might be dangerous for me to share my opinions while still in Venezuela, so I skirted questions and acted amiably throughout the meeting.

Upon my return to the U.S. later that week, I completed the formal report and handed it in to Everett. Based on the fact that there was no system in place to justify the funds, and there was nobody who would be held accountable for allocation and delivery, my report did not support the funding request. As a result, the request was denied by the World Bank.

One morning I went to breakfast with my girlfriends after golf. We talked about our work, relationships, family, and everything in between. Then the discussion turned inward, to making positive changes in our own lives. I shared my experiences in Guatemala with the group, telling my friends that out of these experiences came a desire to make a difference around the world. I wanted to create an organization that would help people in every corner of the earth, solving problems by providing those in need with recycled goods, starting with education supplies. I had no idea how to go about starting this. My friends were very receptive to this idea. One by one, each offered a contribution to my budding project. Then I told them about my recurring dream about standing in the desert and the airplane. My good friend, Janet Barbrick, said "well why don't you call it World Care like your dream? I replied "That sounds perfect."

    While I worked during the day at the hospital, in the evening I began putting ideas down listing what I needed to do to finalize the idea. For a year (1995) I spent my free time educating myself on the non-profit world. It was enormous. The U.S. alone had over 1 million organizations considered non-profit. It seemed like the Red Cross and Religious Organizations had corned the market but, "as I learned" I worked for several hospitals that were non-profit but they never exposed themselves to the public that way. Janet, who owned a printing business, agreed to help with promotional materials. Nancy Schenk, a CPA working for the Nature Conservancy and other non-profit organizations, offered her knowledge in these areas. She explained that I should create a non-profit entity. So I filed the necessary paperwork such as a DBA (Doing business "as"), non-profit business license and tax documents to start World Care in Arizona. With my part-time evening project underway I felt that I was in a place in my life where I could give back. Little did I know what I was getting myself into.

CHAPTER ELEVEN

Déjà Vu

I had successfully completed two full years at UMC. I had been instrumental in turning the radiology department around, streamlining processes and personnel to maximize efficiency and improve productivity by the end of 1996. My budget cuts successfully allowed for the integration of new programs to bring in additional revenue. In two productive years at UMC, it never occurred to me that my job could be at risk.

But the world of health care was continuously evolving and changing, for better or worse. With rising costs of procedures, salaries, and doctors, hospitals were constantly trimming edges to cut costs. Administrators with power began to flounder for ways to save their jobs, using whatever means necessary to secure their position and salary, even if it meant laying off valuable employees. It was only a matter of time. I was devastated and angry; I had many questions but no answers and felt used.

Fortunately, within one week of being laid off, I was offered a job as a project manager at a radiology technology computer software development firm in town. Angels were watching over me, or maybe I really was a valuable asset that

UMC mistakenly let go of too soon. This was the beginning of a major transformation in my life.

Although I preferred the medical field over the software field, my new job was going well and the less strenuous scheduled allowed me to spend more time at night on World Care. I devoted a few hours every night to fleshing out ideas for transporting school supplies to needy children around the world.

I continued to record my dreams and search for their meanings. I didn't realize that my path was already set. It just wasn't what I'd expected. I spent a lot of private time trying to talk with God, but his line seemed to be busy. I would often pace through my backyard, looking up at the stars, hoping for an answer to fall out of the sky as to what was going on around me, my dreams, everything. Finally it came to me, loud and clear, "Lisa, you must have patience." I looked around to find its origin and realized that I was alone. I figured that was a sign that I was ready for bed.

Four months into my project management job, the company was sold and liquidated, and I was unemployed again. I couldn't understand why this kept happening to me! I had spent the last seventeen years of my life working, eating, and breathing radiology physics, only to be laid off again, and again, and again. I tried to stay positive, but this time I felt defeated, and it became a very dark time for me.

I retreated to my home, taking long walks, cutting friends and family out of my life. I didn't want to tell my mother that I was out of a job yet again. I was ashamed of myself because I felt like a failure. Each new job was another failure in the making. Self-doubt set its claws deep in my veins. Fear and unhappiness knocked at my door. I had nothing to show for all of the hard work I had done. I felt I was worthless. For the first time in my life I had no plan; I'd lost control, direction, and self-worth.

After my last day of work, I drove west toward home, and then kept going for hours out into the desert. Not realizing how long I'd driven, I ended up in nowhere, Arizona. I parked the car and began walking in the desert. It was a beautiful afternoon, not a cloud in the sky. I looked up to see birds soaring free, clear over sand dunes. Frustrated with my situation, I cried out to the universe, "What do you want from me? What have I done to deserve this? I need answers. I need help here. You are so big and vast, yet you do nothing to help me." I looked around at nothing in particular, perhaps searching for an answer I knew I wouldn't find. I was surrounded by mountains in the middle the desert and was lucky no one was around to hear my rant.

I began to sob and then I heard a voice, "Oh, you know better than that! Your ego has gotten the best of you. Despite your struggles, you are still succeeding. Your lion has come to challenge you."

The feeling was so familiar; I felt as though I had been there before. Then I recalled a dream I'd had on Easter morning in 1995. It had been three years since then, and yet my memory of that dream remained vividly clear.

I was walking amongst pillars of mountains on a plateau, when a brilliant light from the sky consumed me. I felt as if I were on a quest as I looked forward to the top of the plateau to which I was heading. Then a lion appeared in front of me. I awoke with that image burned in my mind.

I started to look around to see if there really was a lion was in front of me when the voice began again.

"You must set your ego aside and to find your true purpose. You must use what you have learned already. You will be given what you need when you need it most."

At that moment, I thought for sure I had gone off the deep end. I wiped tears from my eyes and started walking back to my car. I was not only metaphorically lost, but literally lost, as well. I had no idea where I was. I'd made random turns and choices up to this point in the vast desert, and now I had to turn around and find my way back. I barely found the strength to make the drive back. Somehow I managed to find my way back home. I felt a sense of relief. Life was going to lead me along bizarre roads to strange places, but somehow I'd be ready for whatever was in store.

I started to recognize that my dreams were clues pointing me in the direction I needed to go, as well as a gift from a source that commanded respect and obedience, from something or someplace beyond my understanding of reality. As I gained more confidence in allowing my dreams to guide me, my insecurity about letting people in on my guiding light kept me quiet about my path of enlightenment. My vision of World Care had come to me in recurring dreams. In the end, if and when World Care succeeded, only then would I consider letting anyone know that I was taking my cues from my night thoughts that made no sense to me at the time. I thought that was a good plan but was it?

CHAPTER TWELVE

You got to have Faith

I have never considered myself a religious person. When I was a teenager, my mother told me that God is for everyone, and that nobody needed a middleman to talk for him. I suppose this is where I found my faith in the universe. Despite the hardship my mother endured as a child, later in her life she always carried a sense of faith with her. She was raised Catholic and had converted to Methodist when she married my father. She recognized always that God had a plan in which she had to trust. It was almost as if she was born with a sense of faith. My life experiences awakened the faithfulness in the universe my mother ingrained in me from a young age. It's not about church, or religion, or fasting - it's a matter of trusting in the universe.

I began to accept the gift of my path—I was meant to build World Care. Recognizing my new calling was difficult on some levels I was grieving the loss of my medical career which I loved, for which I had worked so hard for so many years to establish. World Care, once a part-time evening project, was now my primary focus, and I had a passion to build and protect it. I needed to harness my energy and direct it appropriately to my vision, which would require much creativity, knowledge, and planning, with little room for error.

Getting from point A to point B seemed like an impossible journey. How was I going to expand World Care to the scope and magnitude predicted in my dreams? I understood I had a path, but the mission still wasn't quite clear - my purpose, my life, my future - I needed to find more answers to this burning question. After all, I had jumped through many hoops to get ahead in radiology, only to end up without a job. Now I was holding onto even less professional stability by going it alone. I was building something out of nothing, or worse even, out of a dream. I was overwhelmed by so many changes coming at me at once - the beckoning dreams, my failed career, and most of all changes inside of me - a desire to be bigger than myself, to save the world with school supplies and putting funding and effort where it belonged. Novel thinking, sure, but my brain was running on overdrive.

The Big Leap of 1997

With no income and only a modest severance from the hospital and savings in the bank about $60,000, I stopped asking "why," put a budget together and began working on World Care full-time. I surrendered to the fact that my life was not my own and that I needed to make this contribution to the world. Creating the basis was only the beginning. I continued diving deeper and researching the working of non-profit organizations. The mechanics of running a non-profit is one of life's greatest mysteries. How could an organization exist without a profit margin? How are employees paid? What types of donations are needed to simply keep the organization afloat? I had heard of corrupt administrators in the non-profit sector, and having dealt with the dirty laundry of the health care industry, I was hesitant to proceed into a sector that might be equally tainted. World Care didn't belong among organizations known for taking loads of money from people, with little to show for its income. I knew in my heart that there had to be another way.

The true and good purpose for non-profits is to provide humanitarian assistance to the less fortunate, about this I was certain. I needed to determine how World Care was going to fit into this world, and whether or not it would duplicate an already existing organization, or alternatively, forge new ground in humanitarian aid work. World Care's mission was to get people the help they needed by distributing unwanted supplies from one sector of the world to another, thus relieving need while reusing resources. The method to accomplish this admirable mission was yet to be determined.

Since I had opted to build my own organization from the ground up, failure was a clear and present danger, so I developed a contingency plan in case World Care never fully materialized into something tangible. I made a conscious decision to put 110% into World Care. Make multiple plans and put my energy out there. If I failed at launching World Care, I would try to recover by going back into medicine and finding a job elsewhere. As a precautionary measure, I kept sending out resumes, hopeful that someone would recognize my potential, just in case. The risk of failure was worth the lure of potential success. The amount of goodness that would result from building my vision of World Care would be immeasurable.

Ironically, while working in radiology, my boss had told me that I would never get paid what I was worth without a college degree, although I had made a living without a degree for close to twenty years. After graduating from college, I was rung through the ringer of three jobs and subsequently let go from all. It was like some sort of domino effect and my ego was the last domino to topple. At least out of my bruised ego came a sense of self-reliance above all else. I reeled myself back from self-doubt and focused on building World Care. Paradoxically, building an organization from the ground up gave me a sense of job security I hadn't felt in years. After being laid off so many times, I'd finally found a way to avoid one more. I was my own boss, my own guide. If I failed it would be my failure, my money, my time, my energy, my idea, my plans. I could live with that.

I spent hours in front of my computer in those formative weeks, envisioning World Care as a giant physics equation, making sense of it in my mind. I played with some probability analyses of the cause and effect of World Care's purpose, and how it could impact the world. The workings of World Care started with the laws of physics. Everything has a cause and affect. Every action has an equal and opposite reaction.

I applied literally hundreds of equations to various aspects of World Care to determine the organization's functionality in the world, and found that two important sayings summed up the practical implementation of Einstein's formula, $E=MC$ squared. One of Einstein's great insights was that matter and energy are really different forms of the same thing. Matter can be turned into energy, and energy into matter. For my purposes, that translated into people taking action; converting mass into energy and speed.

Without delving too deeply into subatomic particles in radioactive decay, it deserves mention that when Einstein was building the atomic bomb, he recognized that the only way to destroy matter is by using equal and opposite antimatter. Likewise, if World Care could combat poverty with our waste factor-- recycling reusable good that would otherwise become garbage- -World Care could effectively resolve a moderate portion of our world need. After plugging in some numbers, it seemed like a practical approach to a very big problem. It worked in my head. The question remained would it work in the real world?

World Care needed to go to the next step, it needed space. I had created the basic structure of the organization. The storage facility for school supplies was my garage. I had a small board of directors, a mission, a vision, and a business plan. We were working on obtaining official non-profit status, called the 501c (3) IRS, and had already donated to needy children in Guatemala. The next step was a strategic plan—how to make something out of nothing. If I didn't succeed, I'd have to go back into medicine, and a job where I could easily be laid off again.

I personally designed and distributed flyers, contacted school administrators, attended conferences and trade shows, gave presentations, and held fundraisers. World Care was functioning, albeit struggling. Although we managed to collect school supplies for children in Tucson and Guatemala, getting people to donate money was very hard. Many people were skeptical about giving money to an organization that was new with no community history. It didn't help that United Way was in the news being accused of squandering millions in financial contributions. I was grateful for modest successes and gratified that at least some of our efforts were paying off. I had a deep respect for those who volunteered to help others without asking for anything in return. The volunteers were people whose lives were based on compassion, honesty, love, and humility. They seemed to be at peace with themselves and their surroundings.

The Disaster at the Mall

I decided it was time to do a local collection in order to get the school supplies for the next shipment. I'd gone to see a property owner of El Con Mall, who agreed to give me some space to have a collection drive. I then contacted the news stations in Tucson to see if they could help get the word out about the event. They agreed to do so. I was given two days at the mall and was enthusiastic about the radio coverage from 94.9 KMXZ, and

Channel 9, the ABC affiliate, had also given us some television coverage. The Arizona Daily Star, a local newspaper, agreed to print a few words about the event. With all of this coming to me as donations, there was very little cost to put on the event. I printed flyers and posted them around town.

My goal was to collect school supplies for local kids in Tucson, just as I had done for the children in Guatemala. The malls rules were that I had to be at the mall during regular hours. I assembled the table, table skirt, a box for donations, and two chairs. As the doors opened, there were only a few people walking in. I was foolishly optimistic. Whoever they were, I thought they may be here to support "Tools for Schools." As time wore on, three hours had passed and no one came up to the table. The clock kept ticking away. Then, a person finally came up to me, -but only to ask where "The Gap" was. Into the late afternoon on Saturday, I became the information desk for El Con Mall. By the end of the day on Saturday--from mall open to mall close, sunrise to sunset - I'd collected nothing. I asked myself, was I doing the right thing? I packed my things and headed out to my car, saddened that I hadn't collected anything. I'd spent the entire day educating people about the mall. I had become well versed in that area by 10 p.m. I convinced myself that I had one more day to succeed and Sunday would be a good day for donations. Saturday was a chore day, anyway, I thought. I reflected on what I was doing, and didn't lose sight of the efforts I'd made. Tomorrow would be a better day, I thought.

On Sunday morning, clouds rolled into the sky. It was monsoon season, and by the time I arrived at the mall, rain was pouring down in sheets. Absolutely no one but me walked through those mall doors. I decided that I needed to have a chat with God. I borrowed a pen and piece of paper from a retail shop and began to write a note about my feelings. I couldn't afford to show negative emotion. In the middle of my writing, my cell phone rang. It was Channel 9, asking how things were going. I told them that I'd collected nothing. The man on the line was shocked. He asked if would be okay for the station to come down and do a live story to possibly generate some traffic. It was still raining buckets. Two hours had gone by, and I was losing hope. I had five hours left before mall closing. The news reporter with his cameraman showed up a mere ten minutes later. He staged the spot: "All you have to do is bring in school supplies and put them in this box," and it was live at noon. I was happy to know that someone had come to my rescue. I didn't want to leave with nothing. The next two hours, however, were brutal. No one showed.

Finally, at 3:30 p.m. a woman came up behind me.

"Hello," she greeted me warmly, "I thought you could use some of these supplies." She handed me a packet of loose leaf paper, a pack of pencils, some pens, and a few erasers.

I was shocked. "Well, you can go ahead and put them in the box." I handed her some literature. I felt modestly successful because I now had school supplies for one child. My spirits began to lift. The next hour and a half passed more slowly than the last. I'd had my rush. I packed up my things and left at 5:00 p.m.

The next day I learned that the woman who'd brought the supplies was actually a mall security worker who had seen me on the video cameras for the past two days. Noticing that I wasn't collecting anything, she alone contributed to my collection. Despite the mall disaster, I held onto the hope that these collections could and would be successful in the future.

I awoke each morning, thankful for my gift, and increasingly dedicated to my calling. I still had more questions than answers, but developing any organization takes time. The path is not always a straight and narrow one; I sometimes felt I was forging a path invisible to everyone around me. And yet, I wasn't alone. I had the support of many volunteers, friends, and family.

My dream of standing on a sandy tarmac, beside a "World Care" airplane was becoming a reality. Although World Care's growth was slow and steady, I was constantly battling my inner critic, hard-wiring myself for failure and setback at every turn. I felt something that could only be compared to a maternal instinct to nurture this organization and watch it grow. Like a hen retreating to her coop to guard her eggs, I became a bit of a hermit. I avoided people with judgmental personalities, the type who would undoubtedly question my path. Was I doing the right thing?

Several months after World Care became a full time venture, I was faced with diminishing funds. I had taken a leap of faith and dipped into my savings and retirement accounts, and I was facing losses. This was the first time I had ever gone without income for more than one week. Self-doubt lurked in the dark corners of my mind, challenging the optimistic façade I maintained on the surface. Had I made the wrong choice to follow this dream? Should I have listened to all the people who told me how crazy it was to give up my career in medicine in order to help people, and for nothing in return? I put aside this uncertainty and kept myself busy making plans and finding solutions to one worry at a time.

First, my budget was dwindling. I needed to generate a little money so that I could pay my bills. At the same time while working diligently on World Care, I continued sending out resumes. Despite dozens of submissions, I couldn't find a job. I'm not talking about another Radiology position, but a basic service industry job, a part-time job, even a cashier position would do. As it turned out, I couldn't even get a job washing dishes. A black cloud was following me. I was angry and frustrated with people, medicine, and most of all God. My level of faith was fading fast.

It was late in 1997, and my life had gone from bad to worse. I was exhausted, but still determined.

It had been a very a tough year, full of disappointment and pain, and not only for me. The year was coming to a close and I decided not to go back to Chicago for the holidays because money was tight. Plus, I still had to put together World Care's first fundraiser at the mall for Christmas season. Foster Kivel, partial owner of the mall, generously donated space so that I could sell hand painted tiles donated by another company. For the first time, money was coming in to help pay for World Care expenses.

That fall, my little sister Pam asked me if she could live with me for a while after going through a break-up with her fiancé. Pam offered to help with the bills while living at the house. It's funny how our unpleasant experiences and search for happiness bring about change. I was so grateful for Pam's suggestion and welcomed her idea. I had left home in Chicago when Pam was only eight years old, so I had never really known her as an adult. This was a wonderful opportunity for us to help each other and bond as sisters, and it removed a great deal of financial pressure as well.

Things were looking up, and the holidays were approaching. Then six days before Christmas, my twin sister Cathy's husband died suddenly. After flying home to attend the funeral, I sat with Cathy outside of my mom and my stepfather Peter's house, in the bitter cold of winter. We were angry, exhausted, and crying. Cathy turned to me and said, "I can't wait for this year to be over." I couldn't help but pray that we were both on the brink of pivotal changes in our lives.

CHAPTER THIRTEEN

Momentum

I started the New Year slightly depressed for obvious reasons, although I was genuinely happy that my family had pulled together during this time of crisis to make the best of a bad situation. I thought about my twin sister and what she was going through, although I was unable to ease her grief. We were both hurting, she much more than I. I wanted to be strong for her so I kept my emotions below the surface. I was also grateful to have my sister, Pam, living with me at the time. Even though she kept to herself, I was comforted by her presence.

A Very Hungry 1998

I put everything I had into World Care and was left with nothing-I had no social life, no one to turn this around for me. No one to commiserate with over a margarita; no one to turn to for the answers I needed most. I was failing all by myself. I stopped playing golf, seeing friends, or engaging in anything that required money. Out of such dark times, I became determined to work hard everyday until I had figured out the right formula to make World Care successful. The other option was giving in to failure, and I wasn't ready for that yet.

When I realized that paychecks would not be coming to me anytime soon, I started cutting back on life's luxuries with each passing month. Between living with my mother and my military training, I had mastered the art of discipline. No golf, no gym, no movies, no travel. Instead of buying gifts, I made them. No haircuts, no cable, no gardener, no bug service, no newspaper, no eating out, no new clothes or buying of any kind. The small savings I had was running low. I had barely enough money to cover my mortgage, utilities, car, insurance, and basic food for the next three months. More money was also going out toward getting World Care going than was coming in. I had to survive the holidays and find a part-time job somewhere. As weeks passed, I was no closer to a job, no closer to moving forward with World Care. I was angry and frustrated, mostly with myself.

More cuts were in order. It's amazing how many goods and services we keep in our arsenal that we can do without. The next cuts were health insurance, retirement account, and then savings account. I still fell short. I reassessed my food budget and was able to scrape enough money from my change jar to pay for my $3.00 enforced food allowance each day.

My budget cuts and spare change lasted me until June, 1998. Suffice to say, I never became stick thin living off of pasta, tomato sauce, and ground beef, but I'll save that for my next book. Actually, I always loved cooking, so the challenge of eating on $3.00 per day presented the ultimate challenge of crafting unique, healthy meals on such a meager budget. I remembered the dishes Mom would make out of limited ingredients.

Breakfasts of Champions, Dinners of Paupers

I started my days with Cheerios and toast for breakfast. Lunch was always Ramen noodles, and dinners consisted of a learning curve, beginning with hamburger meat with potato chips, then chili, then spaghetti, then meatloaf, then Hamburger

Helper and finally shepherd's pie. I could make all of these meals with a box of cereal, a loaf of bread, Ramen noodles, one dozen eggs, two pounds of ground beef, pasta, a can of corn, beans, tomato sauce, spices, and one onion. All together, my grocery list cost me about $15.00 per week.

Eventually I stopped using heat and air-conditioning in my home unless absolutely necessary. I brought my work to the library to avoid cooling my house in the 110-degree Arizona heat. At the time, gasoline for my car was cheaper than heating and cooling my home. I inventoried all of my furniture to see what I could sell off to pay bills. Nothing was sacred anymore. I realized that most of my material possessions really didn't matter as much as I thought. I kept essential items such as dishes, my couch, my computer, art supplies, and my car with over 110,000 miles on it. The items that I held onto were only those things that I felt I needed to develop World Care.

Since I could not get rid of the in-ground pool in my backyard, I cancelled pool service and cleaned it myself, saving about $75 each month. Everything else was negligible. I took long walks to exercise and to meditate. When I became fatigued from working, I would take a short, hot shower (another luxury), and read a book to fall asleep. I had faith in my nagging dreams, and I wasn't ready to give up hope.

Despite growing interest in World Care, including news coverage, I was still struggling personally. Money was running out even with my strict budget. Over my years of hard work in the medical industry, I'd grown accustomed to many creature comforts. I felt justified living my well-to-do lifestyle, because I had worked hard for it. But now I was working hard and nowhere closer to making ends meet. I was giving up on creature comforts, sacrificing the life I once knew, those things I thought I couldn't live without, for the sake of my World Care dream.

I didn't want to lose my house and have to live out of my car. I didn't want to have to expose my failures to my family and the few friends that I had by asking for help. I decided to have another chat with God. Maybe I'd find my answers there.

At times I felt like quitting. I couldn't understand how people did not seem to care if children were starving and couldn't go to school, or have clean clothes and water and be free of disease. I considered all of the time, energy, money, and rejection I'd endured for my dream and the fact remained--nothing was bringing this dream closer to fruition. It was like pouring water out of a bucket and getting a drop in return. Why didn't anyone care, and why was I doing this? I told God that this was too big of an endeavor for me. The responsibility needed to be given to someone with lots of money. I wasn't now and would never be that person. The people in Tucson seemed set in their ways with waning interest at best. Though I felt like a failure, I wasn't ready to throw in the towel.

When the negative chatter in my mind finally took a break, I began to realize how many challenges I had already overcome. The universe had answered. My perspective shifted, and I noticed that World Care was growing, albeit slowly. I just had to be patient, believe in my mission and continue my work.

My daily routine began at night with dreams that continued to guide me through the process of developing World Care in my waking life. After my morning physical exercise, I would make a pot of coffee, shower, dress, and retreat to my home office where I would devote my time phoning and putting together fundraisers and defining World Care objectives. I could write and make phone calls to businesses, develop processes to formalize the structure and purpose of our goals, make posters, pamphlets, and letterhead until ten or eleven o'clock at night, seven days a week.

In 1997, I hadn't recorded any dreams in my journal. I realized that many of the dreams I'd had in the past several years seemed to have some connection to my present reality, but at the time I was too exhausted to try to analyze them. I began to add meditation to my daily regime. I felt very connected to God, especially during meditation when I let everything else on my mind go. Sitting quietly to meditate was a good time for me to expose my inner quandaries to the universe. Sometimes, I received answers, other times, modest revelations.

Despite spending most of my time in isolation from the world outside of my door, I always felt that someone or something was with me, guiding me either through my dreams or meditations.

Foreboding Dreams

It was during this time, while still struggling to interpret my dreams that I was finally able to synthesize the verbal messages that often came with the images in my dreams. As I meditated, messages would come through – mostly phrases that had little meaning to me ‐ and I would jot them down at the end of the session. I recognized that the thoughts were not my own because they seemed to have a more formal dialect than my standard American accent. Rather, this voice had a distinctly British intonation, and so I couldn't figure out how it could possibly be an extension of my voice. It had to be someone or something else.

As I wrote the messages in sequence, they began to make sense. As I meditated, I understood the messages to be pure statements of knowing. I felt that some of the messages channeled to me had also been sent to others. The messages were sent to help me interpret my dreams, which would eventually help more people around the world. Each dream was a lesson meant to explain why certain things happened in the way that they did, and to see beyond trivial matters and focus on the big picture.

The dreams and corresponding messages I received over a three-year period of time led to World Care. I believe that our world is constantly changing and consciousness is expanding. I sought solace by sharing my dream messages through the creation and implementation of World Care, while still in its infancy as an organization. Yet I continued to remain silent about the predictive nature of my dreams. I couldn't reveal the source of my knowledge without risking support for the organization. I knew that many people would think I was crazy if they knew that I was letting my dreams guide me through life.

I found peace in painting, drawing, reading, driving, and walks along which I could communicate with the universe. I could chat with the universe any time I was alone. It felt good to open up about what was happening in my life. Our chats weren't always peaceful though. Often, I was angry and frustrated with the changes in my life that were out of my control. I wanted answers and stability. But each time I felt ready to give up on my dreams, a new dream or message would encourage me to continue on my path.

I took long walks in the Santa Catalina Mountains, within minutes from my home in Tucson. To my surprise, I noticed something I had never seen before. The mountains were beautiful, with purple and pink hues reflecting off the shimmering wetness after the rains, revealing flaws and imperfections each one unique from the next. I breathed in all that beauty and wonder, and yet I wasn't able to take it all in. I was losing momentum and feeling resigned about my personal challenges. Every time I came up with a possible solution to my financial problems, nothing resulted. Despite the beauty surrounding me, despite messages about the bigger picture, I still felt lost.

It was a constant battle to shake the negative thoughts in my mind. The disciplined athlete in me made some headway, dragging me out of bed in the morning for long runs through the desert. While running one morning, I recalled an incident from my past in the military. I was climbing to the top of a cliff. When I was almost there, I reached up to place my hand in a crevice when I saw a curled up snake occupying it! I froze in position, looking swiftly for other options. There were none.

"Private Hopper, what the hell do you think you're doing?" my Sergeant yelled at me from below.

I screamed back, "Sergeant, there is a snake in the crevice. I can't climb!" I looked back at the snake. It could've been menacing or minding its own business, I couldn't really tell. I reviewed my options again.

Then suddenly, without really thinking it through, I pushed the snake out of its space and into the air, and with a rush of adrenaline, quickly climbed to the top. I had found the courage to move through my fear and accomplish my goal. I needed to once again summon that inner strength to surrender to what fate has in store, and move through whatever it is I feared.

Part of surrendering involves accepting help. Although my view of organized religion was skewed in a negative way by the greed of television evangelists and clergy who took advantage of their followers, I had the deepest respect for people who gave of themselves without asking for anything in return.

I resolved to apply new discipline to my daily life--to open my heart to becoming a tool to help others, to model myself after the people who volunteered their time so selflessly to World Care.

I cultivated more discipline for my personal journey as well. I drew more inward and tried to simplify my life so that I could devote all of my energy to my organization. I had faith that the universe would not let me fall, which meant trusting my dreams and messages I'd received as my guide. I had mixed feelings and extreme emotions as I continued on my path, not really knowing where I would be in the end.

One afternoon, I picked up the mail from the mailbox at the end of my street and saw that there was a letter from the government responding to a job application I had filled out. I was offered the job in forensics, which I had missed since leaving Washington, DC. Finally, I thought, my chance to become financially stable again. This would be the money I needed for World Care and for myself.

But I was surprised to discover that I wasn't excited about this new opportunity in forensics. I had filled out dozens of applications thinking that a high paying job would make me happy and make my life easy again. I returned home and sat on the couch, staring at the job offer. What was this all about?

I realized that it wasn't the job that would make or break my happiness or even my success. My ego needed some caressing. I was so bruised from feeling undervalued for my work in medicine. I was surprised to find out that I wasn't really interested in earning more money for myself. I'd learned to make do with fewer material possessions. On the other hand, the job offer validated that I was still needed somewhere. It could have been a dishwashing position and I would have felt the same way. The letter told me that I was not a complete failure. With that recognition, I could move on with my life. As I tore the letter in half, I acknowledged a more important lesson though, that the ego can be very dangerous if your value system and priorities in life are only to please your own self and not to help others.

CHAPTER FOURTEEN

The Pattern Shifts

I continued to work diligently on World Care operations and strategies. I met as many people as I could who were willing to help the cause. I had applied for non-profit status several times by then, but the IRS kept turning me down because the purpose was too vague. By this time, however, the foundation of World Care's mission was firmly rooted. Four programs were in development: Tools for Schools, Tools for Health, Tools for Emergency Relief, and Tools for Earth.

Then World Care got its first big break. The *Arizona Daily Star* featured World Care in an article the very same day that we received our 501c3 status from the IRS, giving us the ability to function as a full-fledged, non-profit organization, and giving companies and individuals tax deductions for their donations. Phone calls began to pour in from students wanting internships, and people in the community wanting to volunteer. Things were now looking up for the organization.

All of my energy was continually focused on the success of World Care, and becoming financially independent was part of that goal. I didn't want my friends and family to bear the burden of what I was going through. The challenge to succeed on my own - to proceed with certainty about an organization that was still so uncertain - proved to be a great one. My family gave me silent strength to continue on; I didn't have the guts to fail in front of them.

I missed working in radiology where everything could be answered with equations. But every time I felt like giving up, going back to medicine and moving far away, more messages came to me, urging me to continue. To entertain my mind, I challenged it by working with equations. I took the project of distributing used school supplies and plugged it into an equation, added some variables, and began looking at it like a scientific theory.

Gradually, other organizations and media groups found out about World Care and offered their help. Tucson's KGUN-TV 9 aired a two-day fundraiser for the "Tools for Schools" program, and World Care received an endorsement from Pima Community College. An organization called Teacher-Parent Connection offered to support the first "Tools for Schools" display for stores, and Earth Tones, a tile manufacturer, came aboard as a sponsor. It became apparent to anyone who hadn't yet noticed, that World Care was making progress when the Salvation Army handed over a school supply collection to us since our program had grown larger than theirs! Then our first international request came in from Mexico, and the University of Arizona had its first "Tools for Schools" Dorm Collection, which yielded supplies for 210 needy children.

I received a phone call from Sister Caridad, of Douglas, Arizona, who requested World Care's help in providing supplies for a Catholic school there. I agreed to help her and she was very kind, assuring me that she would pray for me and World Care. Then unsolicited, but somehow knowingly, she said, "God will guide you." She was right. Things were really looking up, and my confidence in my dreams was growing steadily.

Then, on the night of July 27, 1998, I had a horrible dream that frightened me so much that I awoke shaking in a pool of sweat. My eyes were immediately wide open. I jumped out of bed with a feeling of urgency but unsure where to begin. I paced restlessly around the house as I recounted the dream:

I was standing on the side of the road looking at a city in the distance. The city had skyscrapers and bridges leading to its center. It was a clear day with little noticeable weather activity. I saw a man in a car; he was angrily pushing buttons on a hand-held black panel. As I looked at the city one large building collapsed and a large cloud of gray smoke filled the air. I then looked at the car again and the man starred straight into my eyes with intense fury as he flipped another switch. I then looked back at the city and another building collapsed. I began to yell at the man in the car who was dressed in a long white shirt. "No, No," I screamed. Fire was rising from the smoke. Then I became angry at the man, realizing he was responsible for the destruction. I looked at his car and asked "Who are you?" Then, I noticed his license plate. It read: "Land Fil" with a Greenbay Packers plate holder. It was near rush hour time in the city.

The images of the dream burned even stronger as the sun began to show its rays. As I sat down to draw the dream, I tried to remember as many details as I could. I was anxious--what was happening? I didn't know what to do. I felt something very bad was happening, or was going to happen, but didn't know what it meant, or even how to go about dealing with it. I felt insecure. I needed to do something, but felt afraid that I would be judged negatively if I told anyone. I decided to tell only two people, one was a person who worked in the newspaper industry and the second was an agent that worked for the government. I not only wanted their opinions, but more than that, I wanted them to know in case my dream came true.

In the meantime, I focused on the positive changes happening at World Care. Things started picking up during the second half of the year. Tucson Newspapers and Newspapers in Education became official partners, and a good friend of mine, Janet Wood, supported a program proposal for nationwide implementation. The Tucson Chamber of Commerce wrote an article about World Care for distribution to 3,500 small businesses. The universe was finally answering my calls for help.

After hearing about the project through the newspaper, students began joining the organization to work on community service projects. World Care's first student intern was Dina Zahngut, whose project focused on the "art of non-profit promotion." All I could teach her at the time was hard work and persistence because I was figuring it out myself through trial and error. Dina came to my house where World Care was operating out of my garage, and helped me put together school packs. She brought more friends who were a tremendous help. Having been in charge of entire hospital departments for over ten years, I knew how to delegate tasks. Now that I could pass work off to volunteers, I could focus more on the bigger picture: advancing the organization as a whole.

Eventually, World Care outgrew my garage because we were receiving such large amounts of donated supplies. I reviewed our finances and figured we could afford to spend $100 per month for rental space. I called owners of properties and tried to negotiate lower rent in exchange for a tax write-off. One property owner agreed and we signed a month-to-month lease for a warehouse on Ohio Street in Tucson. I was excited to have my garage back, and to have a larger location from which to operate World Care. The only down-side to the move was that it happened in the middle of summer when it is hot as hell in

Arizona. One valuable lesson we learned was that crayons melt. Nonetheless, the volunteers weathered the miserable heat and completed the move. I was immensely grateful for their efforts.

By August, we'd distributed an estimated $210,000 worth of donated school supplies to over 6,000 needy students in 22 schools in Tucson and surrounding areas. Pizza Hut Corporation became the first citywide corporate sponsor to assist in a fundraising event for which $1,000 was raised for World Care.

Dr. Paul Enright, a pulmonary doctor from the University of Arizona, phoned World Care, asking if we could use some computers they were getting rid of. I went to meet him at his office immediately, and Pam Pfersdorf, his assistant, greeted me on arrival. I glanced around the office and jumped–the place was covered with bugs. Pam observed my reaction and told me not to be alarmed.

"They're plastic," she noted. "I use them to teach children in the schools about asthma and air quality." I lowered my guard. Paul was "out shopping for junk," Pam informed me, and would be back in the office shortly.

"I thought he was a doctor," I wondered out loud.

"Pam explained," "He is, but he is also a tinkerer and loves to fix things. Computers, medical instruments, you name it. He can make anything work."

After Paul returned, we discussed ideas to provide used computers to children who could not afford them. For a while after this initial meeting we kept the computers at his office until I was able to find them good homes. "Tools for Schools" had now expanded its role into recycling computers.

Slowly, more and more people were contributing and getting involved–World Care was moving forward. I was optimistic, while still a bit haunted by my dream from July 27th. I had another dream in September that was full of equally disturbing images. I hoped that they weren't prophetic.

Another Dream - September 29, 1998

During September, it became obvious that we were already outgrowing our new home. I shared my concerns with Pam and Paul who by that time had joined World Care as volunteers. Pam told me about a friend of hers who owned a paint factory who might be able to provide free space. We went to take a look, and by November we had moved in. The Company gave World Cares' "Tools for Schools" a temporary home to collect supplies. It was located on the south side of Tucson and had air-conditioning, so we no longer had to worry about melted crayons. All of the volunteers got together to help with the move. The owner was a bit eccentric, but he was willing to help, and that was what mattered. Donations continued to come in and we continued to grow.

In November 1998, Tools for Schools began working in collaboration with International Rotaries in Latin America. What began as a personal project of bringing school supplies to Guatemala was fast becoming an official part of the World Care program. After our fourth shipment of supplies to Guatemala, the Guatemalan Rotary Club supplied the shipping funds and honored World Care for their support by providing and distributing an estimated $2,500 of in-kind donated supplies. World Care was going international and living up to its name.

I was finally able to exhale, at least a little. The organization's mission and infrastructure was solid, so I could shift focus to what lay ahead. But I was fighting with the realization that some of my dreams were becoming a reality, and that fact greatly disturbed me. Although I had dreamt about wonderful things that had come to fruition over the course of my life, I was eerily consumed by the nightmare-like dreams I'd been having recently. I felt that I was being guided, but without instruction other than obscure symbols and scenarios from my unconscious. As much as I felt that my inner sight was a gift, I yearned for a normal life of steady income, support from my friends, and job security.

I had worked very hard to achieve goals in the medical field, and admittedly, there were plenty of times when I felt that I deserved to be successful without having to struggle so much. In one fell swoop, my life had drastically changed. Although World Care was doing better financially, I wasn't living the way I had when I was earning a good salary. I wasn't obligated to support a family, or anyone besides myself, so I was doing fine. If making money was my goal, I would've already left Tucson. But I remained, devoting all of my resources to the growth of the organization. Money would come and go, but the fulfillment I felt waking up every day knowing that I was making a difference in this world far exceeded the value of a paycheck. And yet, the path I was on was markedly different from the one where I began. If I'd felt that I had a choice in the matter, an intelligent choice at that, I'd have continued on with the medical career that I had worked so hard to attain. But I had no choice, World Care it was.

But what was I? A founder of an organization, yes, but how did that translate into a career? Was it sustainable? The more I questioned my path, the concept of "career" held less weight than it had earlier in my life. The career titles we strive for are mere status symbols that we believe are important; yet they don't really define who we are. Most people who enter into the arena of humanitarian aid are the same types that enter law school with the belief that the world is a just and moral place, where fairness prevails. Many lawyers burn out because they realize that the world doesn't always work that way, or they just give in and go with the system, putting their original ideals to rest for the sake of their "career".

Something similar sometimes happens in the humanitarian world. I wanted to believe that everybody who works under the title of "humanitarian aid worker" is there to help others in the most honest and ethical ways, without prejudice, and without selfish motives. Unfortunately, I was too often taken aback by the greed and deception of people who were supposedly doing the same work as I. After witnessing this deception, I realized that anyone can give themselves a career title, but the underlying aspirations and motivations to do a particular job-- not the job title itself--is what truly defines our work and who we are.

Understanding true purpose can only be achieved by finding intrinsic values within oneself, and using and sharing those gifts with the rest of the world. We all have many gifts- -some physical, and some mental. Athletes, for example, have physical gifts that allow them to accomplish many achievements throughout their lives. When people have such gifts and they're lucky, they either recognize it in themselves, or someone else recognizes it in them, and helps them foster it. Often, we only see the final outcome of the athlete's hard work, dedication, motivation, sacrifice, and determination. They make their jobs look easy, when really; the road was most likely as long and hard as any other. We don't see the pain, long hours, failed attempts, and constant obstacles to achieving goals.

Recognizing gifts within ourselves enables individuals to find their purpose in this lifetime. It may sound simple, but it's not. Many people begin one career only to find a decade later that their true interest lies in something totally opposite from their learned path. It was a challenge to recognize and be thankful for my gifts. For a long time, I focused on what I didn't have rather than on the wonderful gifts that I possessed inside of me. Why not follow a dream to be an astronaut or a kindergarten teacher? By following instinctive desires instead of burying them below the surface, a person begins to move in a direction that cultivates them, tends to be happier and more content with his or her life. Why not live the dream instead of ignoring it?

Identifying the gifts within oneself isn't an easy task and requires some inner observations. Gifts and the path that you take to exercise those gifts essentially define a person – not his or her job title, political position, financial status, sexual orientation, religious denomination, or race. Wealth is not determined by how much money a person collects in his or her lifetime but by the wealth of gifts set in motion in a person's lifetime. When I stopped feeling bitter about giving up my medical career, and stopped wishing for my life to be easier, I realized inside how truly wealthy I was.

CHAPTER FIFTEEN

A Messenger at the Mall

"November 2, 1998: Hurricane Mitch hits Central America killing thousands."

In one day, World Care was activated and ready to collect and send supplies out to hurricane victims in Honduras and Guatemala. In the *Arizona Daily Star*, Arizona Congressman Jim Kolbe voiced his support for World Care's collection efforts for hurricane victims. This was our first large scale emergency relief effort, activating the second of World Care's four tools programs, Tools for Emergency Relief. At first our collection was limited to medical supplies, food, education resources, and hygiene supplies. After several weeks we were assisting other organizations that were having difficulty shipping what they had collected.

One of the groups that had approached World Care was Tucson Relief Network. They had collected many supplies but were having trouble with the transport. I met the organizers at the facility where the supplies had been collected. The place was huge. It was a square-shaped, two-story white building called the SILO. They had collected tons of stuff, but it was crammed into the building with no organization. I agreed to help under the condition that they allowed me to move my collection over to this tremendous, but disorganized facility, so that I could minimize the driving I would have had to do between our storage space and theirs. They agreed to my proposal, and in late November 1998, World Care began moving its operations to a 17,000 square foot facility on the east side of Tucson, donated temporarily by the Kivel family, local developers, and the Pueblo Optimist Club. This new space was large enough to support collections for local and international relief supplies for Tools for Schools, Tools for Health, and the Tucson Relief Network.

We organized together and our first shipment to Central America consisted of 25,000 pounds of food supplies. Then we began receiving even larger donations and more volunteers. Thanks to my experience running two radiology departments for two major universities, I was able to handle the rapid influx of people and supplies. This was an exciting time for me because I had to be creative and resourceful at a pace I hadn't experienced since leaving the medical field. The *Arizona Daily Star* ran follow-up stories on World Care projects, which garnered still more attention for us.

After the frenzy surrounding our relief efforts for Hurricane Mitch subsided, I returned my focus to our next big fundraising event that had been scheduled to take place in Tucson's Park Mall. The space was donated and it was only after the Hurricane Mitch disaster that I found out *who* at Park Mall was responsible for donating the space - it was Foster Kivel, the same Kivel family that had donated the SILO space! Rather than view it as a coincidence, I took it as a reminder that the universe was supporting our efforts.

World Care was growing, but still more money was going out than coming in. Over three years had passed since I started building the organization, yet there was no income in sight. Every day was long. I would spend eight to ten hours at the warehouse, then go home and sit at the computer writing grant proposals, drafting letters to potential supporters, and topping off the evening by reading about non-profit rules, laws and accounting.

Everything was new to me. I found it difficult to ask people for money because World Care was supposed to be a conduit for using resources that people did not want, and getting those resources to those in need. I didn't want World Care to be about money. I was also having an uphill battle with my faith. I was running out of money, but the requests for supplies continued to pour in. I didn't want to let people down so, for the second time in my life, I depleted my barely recovered personal bank account to make ends meet while begging the universe for guidance. I was making all of the tough decisions and I felt like I was failing miserably at what I was supposed to be accomplishing. I started to wonder if the idea of following my visions was delusional; maybe I should let go and move on with my life.

There was one problem with letting go; however, World Care was important. I had been exposed to other non-profit organizations, and I knew World Care was a different model that truly was needed in this world. So I stuck with it. I seized every opportunity to meet new people and advocate for World Care. It became the reason I got out of bed in the morning. It was all-consuming, just as my medical career had been in the past. I had to convince myself to stay focused on the positive contributions we were making, not on my perceived failures.

We had our Park Mall fundraiser for "Tools for Schools" timed right around the holidays when thousands of people would be passing through the mall doing their holiday shopping. We set up a booth where children could finger paint. We sold non-toxic paint and tried to collect money and school supplies from the shoppers. We didn't collect very much, but people seemed to admire the booth and the children enjoyed the activity. We were doing it the "World Care Way" which meant donated space, donated products, and donated time from volunteers, so we couldn't lose. Enough funding came in to pay some of our bills and even put a little in the bank. A far cry from the El Con Mall disaster of 1997, making my experience at the Park Mall that much sweeter.

During one of the days at the mall, I went to the food court to grab a bite to eat. I was on a strict budget, so the one-dollar hotdog and fries special, it was. I held my tray of food as I searched for an empty seat. The mall didn't seem that crowded, but the food court was packed. Isn't that always the case? Then I made eye contact with a gentleman sitting at a table with an empty seat. He gestured to me that the seat was free, so I happily joined him.

He was wearing a red sweater with a Scottish black hat. He had a gray goatee and his name was Leo S. He spoke kindly of his wife, Virginia, and how much he loved her. I looked down at his hands. On his left hand he wore a ring, bearing the initials L.S. in diamonds and gold. He told me that Bob Hope had given it to him. As he spoke, he asked that I just listen, adding that he knew I needed encouragement and support. I listened obediently, but really only because I thought he was an old man who needed to vent. Leo began speaking about love, life, relationships, and the world. He spoke of kindness, honesty, and support for one another. Then he started telling me things about my life that only I knew.

"Your eyes tell stories and you should smile more," he told me. "Listen to me, what you're doing is very important. You must begin to believe in yourself and to use the tools that have been given to you and those that will be provided to you soon. Everyone has a mission and this one is yours, so stop having pity parties and get to work. You are going to go through a lot in the years to come, but don't ever give negative energy to the world."

He continued on about stories of his wife to whom he had been married for thirty-six years. He spoke of my father and my mother. I started to freak out a little then. He told me of my family, my purpose, my relationships, and his own passion for life at seventy-seven years old. After forty minutes, I got up to leave. I thanked him for his words and he told me to go forward and never look back. He reminded me of my uncle Frank, and as I looked down at Leo's hand again, I noticed that the ring he was wearing was very similar to one that my uncle had wanted for Christmas a few years back, but that we couldn't afford to buy for him then. As I walked back to the World Care booth, the old man's words encouraged me. Who would have thought that in the middle of the mall, over a hot dog and French fries, I'd find motivation to continue on this path? I suppose sometimes messages come to us in strange and interesting ways.

Requests for help continued to pour in and World Care sent another international shipment to an orphanage in Thailand. World Care's name was getting out there, and with it came more support from donors and volunteers as well as collaborations with larger agencies that needed supplies. I was grateful that we were growing and that I had the skills to manage the volunteers and delegate work efficiently.

Through our daily activities, I observed the important role we played within the local community of Tucson. World Care was filling community needs by giving people a place to grieve, to give, and to help those who were suffering. My role in directing the organization's development became clearer and more focused as time passed. My job was to facilitate a place where people could go to receive help and to help others, regardless of age, religion, or politics. Our doors were open to all people who wished to share the common goal of aiding humanity. People could achieve that by volunteering, donating supplies, or giving funds. My motto has always been to value everything, and in this way life will be fulfilled and not wasted. So, I began looking at everything as a tool to create the overarching, positive environment of World Care, as the organization continued to evolve.

During a walk in the desert near my home one day, I reflected on my past. For seventeen years I had worked behind the scenes in all aspects of radiology. I finally understood that this had been in preparation for my life's work with World Care. My character was being refined, tested, and constantly remolded. It came down to tools and efficiency in the end. All tools are potential energy; one must be willing to use a tool or be used as a tool in order to create energy and effect change. However, without potential energy or a willingness to recognize what the tools can do, nothing can change or be created. I began applying this thinking to everything I was doing to build World Care. I wondered how many tools had been set before me that I hadn't recognized previously? I also reflected on what that old man in the food court had told me – that I would be given the tools I needed to do my work. As 1998 came to a close, I felt positive about our growth over the past year.

On January 23, 1999, World Care had its first reception to honor volunteers and community supporters for putting in over 10,000 hours of volunteer time to support Tools for Schools efforts. Positive encouragement never hurts, especially after a challenging year full of change. People all over the world have their faith tested, both within and without the context of religious structure. There is no human being on this planet that lives without being tested, again and again, by the challenges of life. Being tested is a way for people to prove to themselves that they are good, strong, and important enough to inhabit this earth. Challenges foster our growth and development, and build inner strength.

Kosovo

The 1998-1999 Kosovo War was a test to end all tests. Appalling political oppression and human rights violations under Serbian rule resulted in a humanitarian and security crisis for Eastern Europe and for the rest of the concerned world. The crisis stemmed from political conflict. Kosovo had been part of Albania, but Serbia had taken control in 1912. Kosovo's population was 90% Albanian, and Albanians had been living in Kosovo and the Balkans for thousands of years. In ancient times they were known as Illyrians. Serbs came to the Balkans in the 8th century A.D. and to Kosovo after 1912.

Kosovar Albanians had been suffering under the Serbian government for a long time. When Slobodan Milosevic came to power after the fall of Communist Russia, the Albanians began to suffer more. Milosevic closed down the university and the local schools, and then started firing Kosovar Albanians from their jobs and replacing them with Serbs. Kosovar Albanians were denied access to state-run healthcare, and they quickly lost administrative control of Kosovo. University students were arrested for protesting for their rights to be restored. In 1990, the bodies of 180 Albanian men who had been in military service were returned to their families by the Serbian government. The media was led to believe that the young men had all died by suicide or accident. When the coffins were opened, however, it was revealed that all had died by bullets to their backs, and all of their vital organs were mysteriously missing. Clearly, this was not an accident. The Serbian government started the year long Kosovo war in 1998 in order to clear out the Albanian population. During that time, 20,000 innocent Kosovar Albanians died, including women, children, and the elderly. Thousands of other people were never found. The United Nations still believes that there are mass graves that remain hidden. After *Sky News*, a British television news program, reported evidence of mass graves, forensic experts started to uncover evidence that would eventually lead to charges for war crimes. Kosovar Albanians who were fortunate enough not to be murdered, were driven out of Kosovo into Macedonia and Albania.

By March 24, 1999, Kosovo had become a hostile war area, with over 200,000 Albanian refugees fleeing to Macedonia and outlying countries. By March 30, World Care began a large Albanian refugee collection of clothing and hygiene supplies to be sent to the Balkans. By April 15, the number of Albanian refugees had risen to over 900,000. Albanian ports shut down so that no fuel or relief supplies could enter Kosovo from the Adriatic Sea. Here in Tucson, over 4,000 community members provided relief supplies for the refugees through World Care.

By April 25, over $250,000 worth of relief supplies had been collected for Kosovo. Feed the Children, and Adventist Development and Relief Agency, helped provide transportation for our delivery of supplies overseas. By May, major corporate organizations such as American Airlines, Lucent Technologies, Arizona Women's Prison, Pima County Adult Probation, Davis Monthan Air Force Base, and many other local women's, civic, and church groups joined our collection efforts in support of Kosovo refugees.

KMXZ 94.9, a Tucson radio station, did a weeklong campaign collecting teddy bears for the refugee children. A Mother's Day benefit concert was held at the local zoo where teddy bears and over $20,000 were collected. By the end of June, in partnership with Adventist Development and Relief Agency, we shipped 40,000 pounds of supplies to Kosovan refugees, followed by another shipment in August which included school supplies.

Our efforts attracted media coverage in Tucson's two local newspapers, and three network television channels. I was a guest on two Sunday morning radio shows advocating support for Tools for Schools and other World Care programs. Our response to the tragedy in Kosovo garnered attention that helped World Care receive more community support for our non-emergency relief programs, like Tools for Schools.

That fall, our Tools for Schools program distributed more than 7,500 backpacks filled with school supplies to local children at a Tucson mall. By the time school started, Tools for Schools had helped an additional 2,500 children and 100 teachers by giving them supplies that they couldn't otherwise afford to purchase. Then in September, another 4,000 backpacks were collected and delivered to local needy children, and more supplies were sent to over 250 classrooms internationally. Through World Care, a school in Hermosillo, Mexico, received a school bus.

Donations and requests for help were flooding in as volunteers pitched in to meet the demand. World Care was finally functioning at a level that I had only dreamed of, and I was thankful that I hadn't abandoned my intuitive path. It was only the beginning.

CHAPTER SIXTEEN

Integrity and Trust in Myself

World Care continued to grow the following year, helping people locally while also remaining organized enough to respond quickly and adequately to national and global emergencies. On August 23, 1999, World Care went into immediate emergency response mode after an earthquake with a magnitude of 7.8 on the Richter scale hit Istanbul, Turkey, killing more than 15,000 people with another 20,000 missing. In conjunction with the University of Arizona Turkish Student Association and Circle K International (a humanitarian arm of the convenience store corporation), World Care organized a citywide collection of emergency supplies.

The students in the Turkish Student Association acted as liaisons to various organizations in Turkey with whom we collaborated, including International Blue Crescent. World Care facilitated $250,000 worth of medical supplies that were sent along with 26 pallets of general relief supplies to the people in Turkey who were without food, water, shelter, and medical care after the earthquake.

The Turkey relief effort took place at the same time as our Tools for Schools collection which was scheduled for the end of August, before students returned to school in the fall. While World Care was consumed with the earthquake relief effort, and collecting school supplies, another disaster struck in North Carolina. Hurricane Floyd hit the eastern coast of the United States, causing over $10 billion in damages, and forcing 3.2 million people to evacuate their homes. The death toll reached just sixty, but millions of people were threatened by disease and water contamination as the flood waters continued to rise. In a matter of days, World Care sent over 600 boxes of clothing, shoes, hygiene, and food supplies to a local North Carolina organization called Festival of Hope.

1999 marked a turning point for World Care as the organization gained recognition as a leader in multi-disaster management. Through World Care's response to major natural disasters and international catastrophes, we had earned recognition that had bolstered our collection efforts. But after the hype surrounding emergency relief efforts faded, media coverage waned and donations for local programs began to slow down.

As the year 1999 drew to a close, the political campaigns for the year 2000 were already taking center stage. President Bill Clinton was approaching the end of his eight-year term in D.C. and politicians were scrambling for their parties' nominations. Although I spent close to fifteen years living in the capital, I managed to avoid politics and their polarizing effects.

Meanwhile, the millennium panic was taking hold of the nation and the computer industry was making a killing on software upgrades, as was the generator business. Osama Bin Laden was making headlines, and the Clinton administration was about to pull humanitarian aid funding from Haiti after twenty years of corruption in that country. Tucsonans, for the most part, were more concerned with illegal Mexican immigrants and Arizona-Mexico border issues than what was going on in Washington. The New Year came and went without incident in the "Old Pueblo."

Y2K

We continued our work overseas with Turkey and began a multi-year collaboration with International Blue Crescent, helping to rebuild medical clinics in the regions between Istanbul, Ankara, and Konya. In the final count, the Turkish quake had killed over 30,000 people, and millions more remained homeless. Many organizations and governments promised international aid packages, but those promises were not fulfilled. I decided that I should travel to Turkey to see for myself what was needed and how World Care could help.

I familiarized myself with Islamic culture. I read the Koran, and books about Turkish history, language, people, and the whirling dervishes before traveling. I studied travel guides and mapped out my path around the country. I was investigating for World Care and I knew it was important to become familiar with the culture and customs of each new country to which I would travel. The last thing I wanted to do while in Turkey was to offend any of its citizens who were hosting my visit.

I traveled to Turkey and the Middle East frequently in the late 90's in my attempt to assess the situation and needs. I spent time in fourteen cities and became acquainted with many wonderful people. Each time I returned, I was greeted by more people wanting to work with World Care. I was sought out by heads of states, mayors of cities, private business people, and women's groups. Most of the people that I met were genuinely interested in helping people in the spirit of World Care. But I quickly learned that not every potential collaborative benefactor had altruistic ideals.

Kidnapped

Omar was a friend of my translator in Turkey. I met him one day because he wanted to talk to me about funding a project. Since Omar knew my translator, whom I trusted, I agreed to meet with him at his posh office in the capital, Ankara. We stood on the balcony of his penthouse office, and through my translator, he expressed his appreciation for all that World Care had done for the people of Turkey. I sat down and sipped tea as he continued to talk about the Turkish economy.

He asked me if I could meet him at another site across the city that he wanted to show me. I was scheduled to depart in just under a week, but I told him that we could arrange a meeting with the organization in Turkey through which I was working. Omar didn't like that idea. In fact, he seemed irritated that I wouldn't agree to meet him by myself, and that I wanted to discuss his pitch with the people with whom I was working. I thanked him for the tea, and told him I would contact him the following day. We smiled politely at each other as I left.

The next day, I had a meeting with a large group of people at a local landfill. My translator and I were the only women there. The landfills were located on the brim of the city and were massive. Bloody medical supplies, human waste, animal carcasses, and regular trash were piled up in a giant heap. The smell of methane gas seeped from the ground and permeated the air. Underground methane is like a land mine–it will literally blow up under enough pressure, so I remained on the dirt area and didn't disturb a thing.

The men explained their concerns for the landfill and their need for funding to manage the waste. I explained, as best as I could, that landfill management was beyond the realm of World Care's focus, and that I could not help them with funding. The leader of the group shook his head in disappointment and walked to his car. Then, two men walked me to another car, but not the one in which that I had arrived. By the time I sat down in the car, I realized that my translator had gone in a different car and I wondered if we had been separated deliberately. I felt uneasy as the driver drove farther away from the place where I was staying. I attempted to communicate with the men in the car, but they were unresponsive. I tried not to panic but my pulse pounded as we drove farther out to a place I'd never been.

After several hours, the car arrived at an elegant home and I was escorted inside. Omar, from the previous day, greeted me. My mind darted, putting the pieces together. As I was seated, I searched for clues or weapons (I wasn't sure which) that would help me learn something about the situation I was in. Once again, I was offered tea, which I accepted, but did not drink. I gazed up at the five Turkish men who had joined us in the room. I was out-numbered but remained cool, at least on the surface.

"So, Omar, how can I help you?" I asked.

In perfect English, not in evidence the day before, he told me about a project for which he wanted funding. He reached for a book that was sitting on a table, revealing a gun that was behind it. Oh no, I thought, I'm going to die and be disposed of in the Turkish landfill I just refused funding.

"We are prepared to award you the recycling contract that is being worked on and we need your cooperation along with the World Bank to acquire sixty million dollars, and I need six million dollars from you, off the top," Omar explained, as if it was the most logical idea in the world.

I sat silently for a while, pretending to actually be pondering his offer. The men stared eagerly, awaiting my reply. "Omar, I don't have control over the World Bank. However, I'm willing to propose the project to them once I return to the United States."

Omar told me that the bank in Ankara was willing to put a portion of the money up as a note and he insisted that when we were to appear at the funding hearing the following morning, World Care would be awarded the contract. This guy clearly didn't understand World Care's jurisdiction, nor did he care. He just wanted the money. All I could do was convince him that he needed to let me get back to the United States so that I could work on his project. I needed to get out of there.

Fortunately, Omar agreed with my suggestion, and gleefully gave me a tour of the recycling facilities on premises, which he owned. He told me that his funding portion was to help the soldiers fighting on the borders. The five men disappeared and reemerged as scouts along my tour of the grounds, with automatic weapons dangling from their shoulders. They weren't hunting for deer. The remote environment of Omar's compound was very different from the desert terrain of lower Turkey, which reminded me of Arizona in some ways. Here, the trees were somewhat stubby, so my guess was that we were about 8,000 to 10,000 feet above sea level.

I scanned the area to see what I would need to do if the situation deteriorated. I felt that the best strategy, for the time being, was to talk more with Omar to find where his motivation lay. I agreed to review his plan, assuring him that I would consider the options that he presented to me. As long as he believed I was cooperating, I, acting totally oblivious to our earlier separation, felt I would not be in danger.

I was returned to my apartment around 5:00 a.m. and my translator arrived shortly after to give me the papers for the morning funding meeting. I no longer knew who I could trust. I took a cold shower, dressed, and drank two cups of Turkish coffee.

We arrived at the hearing room. There were hundreds of people from all over the world bidding for the recycling contract.

123

At the front of the room sat a group of contract negotiators and a judge. I could see that the other groups had spent a lot of time and money preparing for this event. I wondered if Omar had approached them as well. With one strike of his gavel, the judge silenced the room. Awards were presented and World Care was named the recipient of the sixty million dollar grant. Every person in the room turned and stared at me in disbelief, wondering who I was. I began to wonder myself what had just transpired. Things felt very wrong.

After several hours of hand-shaking and talking about the next step, I went back to my apartment only to be met again out in front by Omar in a black sedan. It was something out of a James Bond movie, I swear. "I just want to congratulate you on receiving the support from Turkey," he chided. I started to tell him that the contract wasn't any good unless the World Bank agreed to participate, before he interrupted. With a shake of his head, he told me to have a safe trip, before signaling the driver to take off.

The following day I left on my journey home. I felt unsafe all the way to the airport. I wondered if my bags would be mysteriously lost. I wondered if my flight would be cancelled. I wondered if I'd wake up in Omar's compound. My head was spinning. I wouldn't feel comfortable until I reached London the following day.

I felt incredibly lucky to have made it on the plane. I'd gotten this far and was exhausted as I sat waiting for the departure. I drafted a letter to Omar and the Turkish Consulate. I wrote that in good conscience, as the president of World Care, I was forfeiting our project proposal from the sixty million dollar bid award. In support of Turkey's willingness to improve its environment, World Care would be willing to give, "as a gift," the model that we use to help those in need. After I finished drafting the letter, I began to wonder, how many organizations are approached in international settings, and take the money, or are compromised because they do not cooperate over ethical issues?

Less than one month after returning to the United States, I read that the Turkish lira had collapsed to be worth almost nothing, and that the country was in economic turmoil. With guys like Omar leading the herd, I wasn't surprised.

CHAPTER SEVENTEEN

Brother Leo

One thing I loved about my job was that I never quite knew what new contacts I'd make from month to month and where these contacts would serendipitously lead me to find another group of people in need of World Care's support. Brother Leo was one such person who guided me in a completely new direction. And, as his dying wish, he asked of me something I had never endeavored to do before.

I first met Brother Leo in South America while I was conducting needs assessment research for a local Catholic project that had been relatively successful in taking homeless people off the street and providing them with shelter and medical needs. One of World Care's board members informed me that she had been talking with Brother Leo, her elderly uncle, who was a Trappist monk working with poor, abandoned people in Latin America. She asked me if we could help a small but wonderful clinic that was run by nuns in Molina, Chile, where she had traveled that winter. So moved by what she had witnessed, she felt compelled to provide assistance.

A nun named Mother Irene had started the clinic many years ago with only $65, which immediately sounded right up my alley. She'd once found a man tucked into a gutter, with a box over his body. He'd become extremely weak, having no food, and Mother Irene picked up this man and took him into the clinic which began in a home. One by one, they took in more homeless people, even starting a soup kitchen. Through Mother Irene's hard work and determination, she'd managed to care for hundreds of abandoned indigent people, mostly elderly, who had been left behind to die on the streets. The story moved me deeply, and it was just the type of project that World Care could readily take on.

The first step in beginning any project is to perform an assessment, so I went to the nuns to create an overview. They were one step ahead of me though, and their eagerness was refreshing. Mother Irene had already sent World Care an e-mail in hopes of approval for the project. The clinic was preparing to expand its available housing in order to effectively help more people. Supplies were needed in droves, including beds, wheelchairs, walkers, bedside tables, clinic supplies, and more. Funds were needed to cover shipping, and the board enthusiastically tackled that portion of the project. For two months, we collected items for the clinic, and by early spring, we had assembled a forty-foot container of medical resources. By then, the board had raised enough money to cover shipping costs, so off it went.

Mother Irene invited us to come down to Chile to unpack the new equipment and furnishings. World Care was low on travel funds, so I got in touch with friends at American Airlines to maybe pull some strings to help us meet the humanitarian aid shipment in Chile. American Airlines gave us reduced fare tickets which made it possible to fly there.

Molina, Chile

After we arrived at the airport and passed through customs in Chile, a tall, grey haired man in a long brown monk's robe approached us. He gripped a long cane in one of his hands and was surrounded by nuns. He and the nuns began waving excitedly as we came closer. The man was Brother Leo, and he greeted us with hugs. Fortunately Sister Gabriella and Sister Marcela were there to help translate Spanish to English and vice versa making it easier for everyone to communicate with each other.

The drive to South Molina took three hours. The air was warm and dry, and I dozed off peacefully in the car. I awoke before we entered the convent, which was protected by a large white wall. The convent was quite nice, and reminded me a lot of south Tucson. It was a poor community, secured by six foot walls. Coming up the driveway toward the convent, everything was carefully manicured. There were gardeners working, women sweeping, people taking great care for their land. Two dogs protected the front of the convent. As we drove behind the convent, there was a vegetable garden on the left and roses on the right. We passed by some of the buildings where elderly people were housed. We were greeted warmly by a group of nuns, fed a modest dinner, and taken to our sleeping quarters.

Along the way, we passed the day room where nuns were gathered together cutting up sheets, which had been given the convent by another humanitarian organization, but were torn. The nuns were cutting them up into smaller pieces to be made into nurses' uniforms.

Our rooms were modest, each no larger than a 5' x 8' space. There was a single bed, with a cross hanging over it on the wall, a nightstand with a light, and a bible on the nightstand. The bed had a sheet, a blanket and pillow. The small closet had two hangers. Everything was neat and clean, and I felt this was quite comforting compared to where I'd stayed on previous trips. It was more than I expected to be able to stay in a nice, warm room. We shared a community bathroom that was also well kept.

The next morning, after we'd risen for mass, I noticed a large shipping container from Tucson sitting behind the clinic, beyond the rose garden. I recognized the container; it had been sent over a month ago. It was time to get started, the entire convent had waited eagerly for our arrival, and I knew that the next few days of unpacking and utilizing the supplies we'd shipped would be incredibly rewarding. Although I'd traveled to Chile to direct the development of the expanding clinic, something told me that I was about to learn a thing or two myself.

We unpacked and settled in for a few days to complete the job. The setup of the clinic and the new equipment went smoothly enough. The staff and patrons were extremely gracious to be given these supplies and to have the ability to expand their operation. The things that they had asked for were not elaborate, rather basic medical resources which allowed them to get to the next step. We'd sent close to half a million dollars in supplies, which equated to allowing the facility to expand its hosting of the homeless from 30 to 100. It gave way to new lab equipment and basic infrastructure. Beds, walkers, IV-poles--items necessary to meet basic medical needs. It was all about caretaking, not about sophistication.

The walls and floors of the hallways were clean. The beds were perfectly made, even with a person occupying it. The nuns took care of the things that were theirs, and took pride in what they had. Mother Irene had said, "Even though the people are poor, they don't have to live in filth." This was Mother Irene's vision, and I felt a sense of satisfaction knowing that whatever we had given them was going to be put to good use. We thoroughly enjoyed our time at the beautiful convent and were happy to help the kind people of Molina.

Brother Leo approached me as my colleagues and I were preparing to leave, and made a peculiar request. Although I'd noticed Brother Leo observing my interactions over the duration of the trip, this was the first time he'd approached me so candidly. He wanted to know if I would help him write his story about his personal experience dealing with the Catholic Church. I had a million questions to ask him and wasn't sure where to start. What exactly was he asking me to write, and why me? I was a humanitarian with a scientific and medical background, not a writer, but he insisted. I agreed to look over what he had prepared. He seemed convinced that I should be the one to write his story. At the very least, I would take a look. He offered to mail the material to me in the states as we departed, and waved goodbye upon our exit.

I returned home to Tucson and was surprised to find a message from Brother Leo already in my email inbox. He just didn't seem like the type to email, but I was pleased to find out that he was thinking of us and thanking us for our work on the project. A couple of weeks later, I returned home from work to find several heavy boxes from Brother Leo at my front door. I dragged them inside the house where they sat undisturbed until the weekend, when I finally had time to sit and take a look.

I opened the first of three large boxes with a kitchen knife and removed the stuffing from the top. The box was loaded with papers. As I scanned the contents of the other boxes and began to read the documents, I realized that these were papers that Brother Leo had collected over a span of fifty years. There were writings, legal documents, and pictures. I wondered who the people in the pictures were and how those people related to the documents and to Brother Leo. Since I was committed to other projects at the time, it was several months before I could really sift through all of this material. I set Brother Leo aside for a while, until one night when I had a dream urging me to contact him. Brother Leo had recently moved from the monastery in Chile to Spencer Abbey, near Boston, Massachusetts.

A few days after my dream, almost as if he had read my mind, Brother Leo phoned. "Lisa, hello dear, how are you doing?" For a moment I thought it was the actor, Jimmy Stewart on the line, but was even more excited when I found out it was Brother Leo.

"Did you get my packages?" he asked eagerly.

"Yes, Brother Leo, I got them. It's good to hear your voice!"

"Good, good! Did you read them?" He pursued.

I hesitated before responding, "Brother Leo, there are about 5,000 documents here and I'm not quite sure where to begin."

"Well, I'm glad that you're going to help me. It's a dying monk's wish, you know."

I didn't have the heart to tell him I couldn't do it, so I promised him that I would start reading and get back to him as soon as possible.

As I sifted through the papers over the next few weeks, and after a few back and forth conversations, he convinced me that we should meet in person to talk. So, on my next trip to Washington, D.C., I took a detour to Boston where I met with Brother Leo. I brought along the outermost envelope contained in the boxes of documents he had mailed me several months ago. While the airplane taxied, I settled into my cramped seat and retrieved the envelope from my carry-on. Finally, I had time to review some of Brother Leo's paperwork without interruption, albeit only hours before I'd be meeting with him. Attached to the packet of papers was a letter he'd written to me:

> *My dearest child,*
>
> *What you are about to read are the details of the letters and documents that sealed my fate in 1961 after Sarita Kennedy East died. I am giving them to you because I am 87, and an old man, and I trust that you alone can set the story straight.*
>
> *Please accept these as gifts. Sarita would have loved your organization, helping the poor all over the world. If you have any questions, please call. Remember, it is about the truth. I will be happy to answer any questions you have. You must, however, do so quickly. Time is running out. God Bless You, Brother Leo*

I arrived in Washington, D.C. first, for a quick meeting regarding peace talks in the Middle East. The meeting was actually comprised of representatives from various large non-profits similar to World Care in some ways. We came together to discuss the potential of collaborating our efforts in the Middle East. The meeting went well, and after it commenced, I headed back to the airport. My final destination was Boston, where I'd meet with Brother Leo later that same day. At my arrival at the airport, a short elderly man recognized me and politely took my bag. He led me toward Brother Leo, who had aged noticeably since our last visit. He was using a walker, an upgrade from his cane in Molina, and at once I understood the urgency behind his request.

"How are you, dear? Oh, you look lovely. How is everyone?" His breath was labored as we walked toward the exit.

"Everyone is fine, Brother Leo," I replied. "They're all glad that you made it to the States to get support for your health."

The old man who was escorting us hailed a taxi van, and the three of us climbed inside. We drove to a local restaurant just outside of the monastery. We had a quick bite as there wasn't much time to discuss everything we needed to get through.

"Oh dear, I'm an old man, you know. I hope God takes me soon. I can't see anymore and I'm getting a little forgetful. Lisa, we don't have much time to talk, so I'll be brief." He handed me another manila envelope containing more documents.

"These are the last of the documents. I found them going through the last box in my room. It wasn't too much information for you, was it?" He smiled jokingly, and then added in a more serious tone, "Have you had a chance to read anything yet?"

"Not really, Brother Leo, I plan on making time when I return home." I was being honest, but I felt bad that I hadn't gotten to his story. I needed guidance or direction, or maybe I just needed more time.

"Oh, you must," he told me, with urgency in his voice. "I don't have much time left and I would like to have my story told as soon as possible. You're the one," Brother Leo insisted, as he leaned forward, adjusting his robe as he spoke.

We talked at length about the contents of the book he wanted me to write. Everything was truthful, and there was evidence to prove it, he said. I barely needed a reminder of the boxes of evidence, documents, letters, and paperwork that had arrived at my doorstep and currently occupied my home office. He leaned in closer and spoke in a hushed voice, warning me to keep the documents in a safe place.

The Catholic Church would be very unhappy when his story was finally told. He seemed a little too cautious and paranoid in my view, but then again his emotions in discussing the papers were so intense that I couldn't help but obey his wishes. I assured him that I would guard the boxes with my life. At this, Brother Leo was visibly relieved and gave me a warm hug as a vote of confidence. The driver took me back to the airport and I was quickly on a flight to DC. What I had gotten myself into this time?

I opened the latest envelope, the one that Brother Leo had just given me, on the plane. A photo fell out from between stacks of pages. It portrayed a tall, light-haired, handsome, yet modest looking young man, standing in front of a monastery. I recognized the young Brother Leo immediately, the photo must have been taken several years before he'd become a monk. I wondered what it was about his story that had forced him to remain silent for so long.

The Saturday after returning to Tucson, I started going through the boxes he'd sent, reading page after page. Before I knew it, it was 2:00 a.m. I was hooked. For the next five months, I spent all of my free time reading through the piles of papers Brother Leo had sent me, organizing them in chronological order, searching for the reason for his sudden urgency. It couldn't simply be that he was an old man, could it?

As I continued digging deeper into the paperwork, the story began to unfold. Brother Leo's story was unexpected. I couldn't believe all that he had lived through in his lifetime. He was not just a Trappist monk, but one of the most successful fundraisers ever to grace the Catholic Church. His life story and dedication to charity taught me valuable lessons that applied to World Care. I finally understood why he'd chosen me. We were doing the same kind of work, and he had decades of wisdom and experience to share with me and the rest of the world.

Brother Leo's story began in 1960 when he was dismissed from his order and forced into exile by the Catholic Church. The reason for his dismissal was that he had tried to uphold the last wishes of an elderly Texan woman named Sarita Kennedy East who had bequeathed $300 million of her fortune to her foundation. Sarita's wish was for that money to be used to help the poor of the world, but the Catholic Church had other plans. As Brother Leo and Sarita's story came together, I wondered why some people choose, with genuine honesty and goodness, to work so hard to serve others, while others, choosing instead to be self-serving and greedy, do anything in their power to twist the truth to get what they want.

Brother Leo's saga involved decades of conflict and litigation. It's a story of faith and the challenges one faces in defense of truth. The lessons that Brother Leo learned would undoubtedly apply to challenges I would face as I continued on my quest for donations and sponsors to help the poor. His story solidified my already tarnished view of the corruption inherent in many of the power structures of organized religion. Mostly though, I was struck by how the mysterious universal intelligence manages, through intricate circumstances, to bring people together so that they can receive life lessons in order to fulfill their destinies. It's nothing short of miraculous. With the information he gave me and the gift of his friendship, I hope to bring his story to you in the future as there are many more lessons to share. As I sat in reflection, a voice whispered to me. "Follow your inner wisdom Lisa. As you discover your life's work you need to listen to your inner self."

I opened my eyes and walked away with a sense of peace, realizing that creating my life's work is a process of discovery and every time I dream or go "within" will place me on my true path. What I didn't realize was when you open yourself to the universe you expose yourself to everything both good and evil. My question is how do you process the evil?

CHAPTER EIGHTEEN

Nightmare

It was a Tuesday morning, and I was lying in bed, half-awake, thinking about my day's to-do list. IBM had called the day before to confirm that they were sending volunteers over to World Care to help out with our annual Tools for Schools book sorting. I was scheduled to speak at a local church at 9:00 a.m. I was so comfy in bed, but knew I had to get moving soon.

Then the phone rang. "Get up! Get up!" a friend yelled in panic, "Lisa, turn on CNN! The World Trade Center, Pentagon, and an aircraft have been hit in New York, Washington, D.C. and somewhere in Pennsylvania! Get up! Get up! It's a terrorist attack!"

I turned on the television and along with the horror I felt upon viewing the live footage unfolding on the news, was the freakish chill knowing that I had foreseen this event in the nightmare that I had on July 27, 1998 and repeated several times afterward, which made the scene on CNN all too familiar to me.

I am standing on the side of a road. Behind me is a low white warehouse with bars around it. I hear a beeping sound, and then I see moving cars on the road. A man of Middle Eastern descent in a white car passes me and he's holding a black box device. To the right is a large cloud of venomous smoke, it is emerging from a major city. There's an explosion, and a structure collapses. I turn and see the man again; he looks at me and flips several switches. I look back at the city and it is submerged in black smoke. I scream at him, "No!" realizing what he is doing. Then another explosion occurs, I am angry and I look at the back of his vehicle. His license plate says "Land Fil" inside of a Greenbay Packers plate holder.

Despite similarities, this dream did not tell me the exact date and time of the event, so the information didn't weigh the same to anyone else but me, until now. I had sent a description of the dream to the feds back in 1998, but never heard from them. I understand that a million bits of information come across their channels daily, and I'm sure that dream submissions are filed in a "to be determined" folder. Had I been in their shoes, I would have probably filed it there too.

As I watched the buildings crumble, I started making phone calls. It was time to fire up the emergency relief arm of World Care, and start to move in full swing. Since World Care had already dealt with the aftermath of the Turkish earthquake and the hurricane in the Carolinas, we were experienced in disaster relief. Responding to the terrorist attacks in New York was much easier than responding to the earthquake in Turkey, in fact, because we did not have to deal with customs or immigration.

Ground Zero

Also, the benefits of having zero governmental or religious affiliation gave World Care a huge advantage when it came to avoiding red tape and quickly getting help to where it was needed most. The Red Cross, on the other hand, is mandated by Congress to respond to disasters with the oversight of Federal Emergency Management Agency (FEMA), a government entity.

World Care is a part of a small group of non-profits that are made up of civilians helping civilians, and therefore does not have to answer to any bureaucrats or deal with much of the red tape that federal agencies and religiously affiliated organizations typically encounter.

World Care immediately collaborated with individuals and organizations in New York and around the country who shared our philosophy. In Tucson, the local community responded intensely. The leveling of priorities, the assembly of managing volunteers, and the organization of supplies and shipments, flowed automatically because we were managing money and supplies effectively. Within thirty-six hours, we had volunteers at ground zero distributing hundreds of hepa-filter respirators, and assisting in search and recovery efforts.

Our previous emergency experiences and our instincts guided us in the formation of the infrastructure necessary to carry out our mission, and we shared our model with other people and organizations in need of similar structuring. This is another distinguishing feature of World Care – we have a transparent operating model so that others can learn to use it, unlike other "non-profit" organizations that covet their infrastructure as if it were a commodity that, they fear if shared, would weaken the value of the organization. To me, that contradicts the entire point of a "non-profit" organization. I can't help but wonder about the agendas of some of the other organizations who act more competitively than cooperatively.

World Care's experience at Ground Zero confirmed my theory that civilians could manage emergency relief as well as, if not better than, the government. Our organization provided the single largest civilian response to the tragedy, and while trucks under FEMA control were being stopped from entering Ground Zero, World Care's vehicles were escorted by police to ensure that the supplies delivered were actually received. I felt extremely satisfied knowing that the money and supplies we were sending to New York were going exactly where they were needed in a timely manner, and that World Care had been able to carry out the relief efforts without governmental intervention or regulation.

Unlike large relief organizations that retain a "liberty fund" where they keep their excess money, we put the funding to use exactly where donors would expect it to go. World Care puts its resources into existing disasters, and is able to do so because our model is simple and efficient. By collaborating with smaller non-profits and individuals, we provide the resources where needed, rather than using money to pay for the administrative costs of mega-sized government organizations. As a result of our transparent, simple model, and efforts of hundreds of compassionate volunteers, World Care has gained national recognition as a preeminent model for emergency response.

Although this recognition was thrilling to me, it was not so to all. One afternoon toward the end of September, I was managing operations from the Tucson office when the phone rang. It was a person claiming to be the head of FEMA. He told me that World Care had to pull out from our efforts at Ground Zero, to stop what we were doing completely and at once.

I asked him, "Are we under martial law?"

"No," he responded.

I calmly explained that World Care was an organization of citizens helping citizens, and there was nothing he could do to stop us.

He replied, "We never had this conversation," and hung up.

140

So maybe my idea that non-profits and the government should work together to minimize the effects of disasters on society was not one shared by FEMA. But I was optimistic that someday we'd eventually collaborate as more hearts and minds opened to what was truly important.

I couldn't help but notice the parallel between World Care's efforts to help people without the government's approval, and Brother Leo's attempts to provide humanitarian aid without the interference of the Catholic Church. One thing that I have learned throughout my travels and dealings with governments and religious organizations around the world is that they are all essentially businesses, susceptible to corruption. Often in countries where power isn't being used to oppress the governed, structures are in place and resources are in use to maintain the status quo. This could be another book in itself, after the one about dining in for $3/week, of course.

I learned firsthand about corrupt government operation, when I was in Venezuela performing a needs assessment on a hospital in Caracas in the early 90's. Five years after I filed my report on Venezuela, I was to find out from several other organizations who had visited the same hospital that conditions were the same as they'd been years earlier. Like me, they had been summoned to evaluate the dilapidated conditions by the corrupt government who were attempting to acquire millions under false pretenses, claiming the funding would go toward repairing the hospital. I was truly blessed that Brother Leo had shared his experiences and his wisdom regarding the topic of corruption.

The lessons he taught me through his story would no doubt continue to be invaluable for me in the future. After 9/11 World Care gained a tremendous amount of experience which brought more financial contributions from local donors. The World Care formula was modest but working, so in 2002 for the first time since its inception, I was able to hire personnel and fund portions of projects. It was another milestone.

CHAPTER NINETEEN

Haiti

In January of 2003, I embarked on an assessment trip to Haiti. It had been three years since the U.S. government had stopped providing humanitarian aid to Haiti because of massive corruption and political instability. During those three years, a group of airline employees began to make humanitarian trips to the most volatile areas in Haiti, helping children orphaned by the AIDS epidemic that was proving rampant all around the country. It wasn't long before Peggy Clark, an American Airline employee, approached World Care for assistance. We discussed the situation, and agreed that a needs assessment was a necessary part of the process. In addition, we would bring a large haul of food, education supplies, and basic medical products to distribute among the Haitian clinics.

We landed in Haiti, traveling through customs with literally hundreds of boxes of relief supplies. Thankfully, Peggy took charge having previously dealt with this before. Guards with semi-drawn weapons surrounded the area where our boxes were being unloaded. I didn't think I could ever get used to this, but Peggy barely blinked. Several people who weren't part of our group attempted to pull supplies off the load, but the goods were rescued by another aid worker who had arrived to meet us. A growing crowd of locals seemed a little too eager to help us load the supplies onto trucks. The trucks would then take us directly to the clinics and orphanages we were there to visit and assess.

Haiti was a terrible, depressing sight. I had never seen so much poverty in one place. At the time we were there, unemployment was up to eighty percent, and those who did work earned only about fifty cents per hour, some only a fraction of that. Chaos ruled the country. What had once been a fertile, lush, green country with agriculture as its main industry had been stripped of all but two percent of its forested land. As a result, deforestation was one of the causes of the rise in unemployment. Infertile land was more susceptible to landslides and flooding. When viewed on a satellite photo, the contrast between Haiti and the Dominican Republic, each occupying opposite sides of the island of Hispaniola, is striking. Haiti appears parched and dying next to its greener, more affluent neighbor.

We rode into the mountains in a basket truck which was essentially an old truck with an open back and two makeshift walls that were barely able to contain the supplies. The roads were horrible, and we spent much of our 15 mile per hour drive negotiating boulders and meandering cows. We passed endless neighborhood-like vistas, scattered with shanty homes and indigent people everywhere. Hundreds of people at once, bartering with each other to get what they needed to survive. There was no order, no structured marketplace.

We traveled with female shamans for protection, since locals feared being cursed if they tried to steal from us. Amazingly, this was the safest way to travel around the country. Superstition was a far more powerful defense than armed guards. The country was as volatile as ever. Citizen uprisings were taking place in

Port-au-Prince and the government was retaliating against them. Twenty people had already been killed, and many more injured. Many aid projects were cancelled and people were left to suffer as a result of the political and social unrest.

Before the United States pulled their resources out of Haiti, they provided a lot of financial help to the floundering country. But over the years, it became apparent that the corrupt Haitian government never used the funds to develop infrastructure, schools, or hospitals. This corruption had been going on since the eighties when Americans and Europeans were still vacationing along Haiti's beaches. With the advent of the Internet and more international reporting, issues of humanitarian despair and corruption were finally brought to light. The United States responded by withdrawing aid, but individuals like Peggy reacted by doing what they could because so many were still suffering, and with the hope that if aid went to the right places, things might one day improve.

When we arrived at the first of several orphanages, I was appalled by the conditions in which the children were living. Although the community was making an effort to care for their orphans, they didn't have the supplies to do so adequately. The orphanage consisted of an area confined by chicken wire, concrete walls, a dirt floor, wooden pallets for beds, and an open water sewage system. The children were not well. They had swollen bellies, skin diseases, infections, dysentery and malnutrition. The orphanage was bug-infested, with no clean water or basic medical care. Each child had only one set of clothing, and no shoes.

We began at each new orphanage by holding clinics to identify the basic health issues that needed to be addressed. We met hundreds of children who shared varying degrees of illnesses. One evening, while we were stationed at a clinic in the mountains, someone stole the axle off our truck, and left the stripped vehicle on cinder blocks. Instead of moving forward to the next clinic, we were stuck searching for a replacement, which very possibly would turn out to be the one that had been stolen in the first place.

Our next stop was a nice home in a relatively upscale neighborhood. However, we were still subject to rolling brownouts. The government could not meet the demands for electricity. Those people whose homes were not hooked up to utilities attempted to tap into main wires in order to bring electricity into their houses. During brownouts, when the electricity was turned off, they tinkered with the wires to find a free connection. This was a dangerous job and many people were electrocuted in their attempts, when the electricity would jerk on unexpectedly.

Despite the scale of the horrific and seemingly insurmountable conditions in Haiti, we made a good deal of progress with the orphanages. The children were able to thrive with the aid we provided to them. They went from being severely undernourished and disease-ridden to being given all the resources to be healthy and well-nourished. They were given purified water, adequate food, and regular clinic visits, plus medicine and vitamins. This was a continuous process, and until World Care came into the picture, Peggy had been struggling to provide adequate resources. World Care was able to provide the community with all of the needed supplies, and finally their needs were met consistently. Peggy continued to work in the area and became World Care's liaison on the project. Within years, the children were growing into healthy adults, forming families, and beginning to make a difference in their communities.

During our stay in Haiti, I noticed that there were other non-profit organizations trying to help small communities, but failing in their endeavors, because it was too difficult for them to make sustainable changes. I learned that one of the most important aspects to making lasting improvements is consistency of sustainable improvements to health and well-being.

I also learned that sometimes the size of devastation can be overwhelming, but by breaking things down into more manageable groupings, massive poverty becomes less paralyzing. While I couldn't change the political structure of the Haitian government, I could help the children on a smaller scale. Making a difference on the micro-level makes results possible that may seem insurmountable on the larger scale. Bringing aid to an entire nation is an overwhelming task, whereas helping individuals is very doable. While some people said these problems were too big, I said to do nothing is a crime.

Peggy's project in Haiti was the birth of the Project Managers program at World Care. World Care was never about owning our model or coveting our methods of helping people, entirely the opposite actually. Part of World Care's mission is to create models that could be used by other non-profits across the globe. In this way, World Care is about allowing people the resources to participate in fulfilling other people's dreams locally, and around the world.

CHAPTER TWENTY

An Angel in the Air

The 2003 invasion of Iraq was launched by the United States and the United Kingdom on March 20, 2003, with assistance from a loosely-defined "Coalition of the Willing." The U.S. military operations were conducted under the name "Operation Iraqi Freedom." After approximately three weeks of fighting, Iraq was occupied by coalition forces and the twenty-five year rule of Saddam Hussein and his Baa'th Party came to an end.

World Care quickly became involved in the rebuilding efforts, especially in helping women and children by providing education and health resources to communities that had none for over ten years. We collaborated with other NGO's (Non-Governmental Organizations) to provide computer labs for ninety institutions, which helped to rebuild depleted communities. We also provided education supplies to children returning to school, and we were able to accomplish all of this over the course of one year.

In September 2003 I traveled to Iraq to perform a needs assessment and also to follow up on our projects. Because of the

148

ongoing war, I needed to fly into Turkey where my colleagues with a Turkish non-profit would facilitate my entrance into Iraq, via all-terrain vehicle, from the southern border of Turkey. There was no air transportation into Iraq because planes were in danger of being shot down.

Sitting next to me on this flight was a tall, dark, and handsome man in his late thirties or early forties. He introduced himself as Greg, speaking with a southern drawl and always showing a kind smile. He asked me where I was headed.

"Iraq," I told him, "but I'm holding over for a day in London before traveling to Turkey."

Greg wished me a good trip, donned a Bose headset, and became engrossed in a book entitled "A Divine Revelation of Heaven." He held the book with one hand, while the other scribbled notes on a small pad. I couldn't help but notice how tiny his handwriting was and how diligently he recorded notes from the book.

I ate, read for a while, and watched two movies before falling asleep for the better part of six hours. When I awoke, Greg was still reading. About an hour outside of London, while we were eating breakfast, Greg turned to me and asked, very pointedly, if my work had anything to do with faith.

"I hope so," I told him. "Humanity is my focus and not religion. Why? Are you a religious man?" The reasons for my trip became clearer to me as those words came out of my mouth. While faith had guided me to create World Care, it was my concern for humanity and my desire to help people that kept me going.

"Your gift is about to expand beyond belief," Greg told me. He said that he was there to bless me in my travels, and he talked about faith and God's will. "I have nothing to say about myself, only that God has given me a message to give to you. Your journey will be blessed and you will be protected by God." Greg reminded me of the stranger named Leo S., with whom I had sat and had lunch at a mall in Tucson a few years back.

I listened intently, as Greg told me a little more about himself before we landed. He was president of a telecommunications firm. While his business trip had great importance, since meeting me he understood that the true reason for his trip was to meet me on this flight, and give me a message of faith and guidance. While I had slept, he stayed up all night composing what he needed to tell me that morning on the plane over breakfast. He told me that he had suffered difficult losses in his life, and although he had a heavy heart, he still felt filled with love from God. I thanked him for his insights and support for my efforts.

When we reached the gate at Gatwick Airport in London, we gathered our things and exited the plane. Greg and I separated at customs and went our separate ways. I exchanged some money, and got directions for getting to the city and back for my next flight the following day.

I caught the Gatwick Express train to Victoria Station, and transferred to Piccadilly Square on the tube, the Londoners' term for the subway. Within thirty minutes, I was in the center of London. I walked, snapped pictures, and people-watched. I was pleased by how kind and helpful the people were-and with a Starbucks on almost every corner, London wasn't the culture shock I'd imagined.

After I had had enough walking and sight seeing, I hopped back onto the tube and went to the airport hotel for some rest and a bath. I ordered room service, listened to the day's news on BBC, and went to bed.

In the very early morning, I caught a flight to Istanbul, which passed without incident. On the plane, I spoke to an interesting gentleman beside me. He was a retired British officer now working with NATO recruiting medical professionals. I imagined that would be a challenging job right now, with the war going on. We talked about strategy planning, or lack thereof, with the war, and then I slept for the remainder of the flight.

Upon my arrival in Turkey, I quickly learned that the price for a visa had jumped from $45 to $100 – ouch! No credit cards accepted, either. My last trip to Turkey had been in 2000, and I hadn't left under the best of circumstances. For some reason though, I didn't feel too concerned about this trip. When I'd left in 2000 and the Turkish lira fell through the floor, I continued contact with the International Blue Crescent (IBC). I'd written some emails over time to test the waters with the IBC's more recent projects. I wanted to touch base and see if the temperament had changed. I wondered how things had been fostered over the last few years. From a distance, it became clear that Mussafer, one of the founders of the organization, had a good heart. It was a learning curve, and I wanted to work through past complexities. A driver met me at the airport and brought me to meet with the folks at the IBC, the group that brought me to Turkey the first time after the earthquakes.

A couple of new players had joined the group since my last visit. The IBC had also added some more projects to their dossier, as well as a new office. Considering that they had only been working in the charity world since 1998, they were doing well for themselves. Helping many Turkish people in need, their presence was felt not only within Turkey but also throughout the Middle East. It was difficult to gauge how deep their resources ran, but from what I understood, they were a powerful humanitarian organization.

I met with Mussafer in his office and we exchanged warm greetings. We wasted no time, and delved into the projects on which we were collaborating. He reviewed the required conduct that was expected of me, as well as the itinerary for my trip into Iraq. Despite the show of military and friendly people on the Turkish side of the border, Mussafer emphatically explained that there had been an increase in kidnappings of U.S. and foreign aid workers during the last few months. He made it very clear to me that I was entering unsafe territory, and that I had to be vigilant. The U.N. post in Erbil had just been bombed and the U.N. was recommending that aid agencies start evacuating.

"Once you fly to Diyurbakir, a city in the far east of Turkey, a driver will meet you. His name is Bazit Tosun. He has a Renault Toros and will have a card with your name on it. When you approach him, ask for identification and check the license plate. It should read 06 KJ 821. If it doesn't match, walk back inside and connect with a guard. Once on the border, another man will escort you through the process, then your Iraqi escort, Mr. Kamara Bayir, will receive you. Be very careful," Mussafer warned.

We spent another three hours reviewing the projects, plans, and strategies for my time in Iraq. Some important voices joined our conversation, shedding light on women's issues, politics, tribes, and mistakes already made by the U.S. government. I couldn't help but feel compassionate for the women and children of these oppressed Middle Eastern countries, most of whom had no voice in the politics that lead time and again to aggression and war. After concluding our discussion, we hastily ate a traditional Turkish dinner of dried meat and yogurt. There was an undeniable sense of tension lingering in the room due to the prospect of a difficult and dangerous trip into Iraq.

I stayed at the Green Park Hotel in Bostovic, Istanbul. I

didn't sleep very well that night. After a few hours of tossing and turning, I reluctantly got out of bed at 4:00 am and began writing in my journal. My mind raced with dreams of the coming days. I wrote down everything I could remember, knowing that the messages could very well be helpful to me in the near future.

The next day, I exchanged more money into Turkish lira to cover the cab rides and any other incidentals I might encounter. I picked up the local newspaper and read a story about a young teenage girl who had been murdered by her father on the way to the airport. The girl had apparently "dishonored the family" by arguing with her father, for being too Westernized, and for having a boyfriend with whom her father suspected she'd been having a sexual relationship. Apparently he didn't like the fact that his daughter was turning into an independent person with a mind of her own. What sickened me the most about the story was that this was not an isolated incident.

For centuries, Muslim women have suffered under the single-sided laws of the male dominated Islamic world. "Honor" killings, the tradition of stoning women to death for adultery or fornication, continue to occur in fundamentalist Muslim countries such as Saudi Arabia, Iran, and parts of Iraq, as well as in some Hindu and Sikh societies, and the perpetrators are rarely punished. Yet, murder and torture are not endorsed by the Koran or any authentic spiritual teachings.

Unbeknownst to most Americans, these types of murders are even happening in the United States and in Great Britain. One thing they all share in common is that these crimes happen mostly within communities that are uneducated. That's the main cause of the problem.

Education is a major part of the solution to human rights and equality. Millions of people are denied education, employment, and the right to pray. Education is the key weapon with which the women are fighting back and slowly receiving a long overdue response from the international community.

The time was ripe for barbaric regimes like Saddam Hussein's Iraq to be questioned. Yasmin Alibhai-Brown, a Ugandan born, London-based journalist has stated, "All cultures have aspects which must be allowed to flourish; all cultures also have practices which must be openly condemned." The inhumane treatment of women in some fundamentalist societies is one such practice that ought to be condemned, especially state-sanctioned imposition of suffering. While women in the Muslim world slowly make advances, the story of their plight must not be forgotten. The crime of genital mutilation is still carried out on close to half a million children a year, and schoolgirls in radical Muslim countries can only rebel against such ludicrous, hateful laws by committing suicide.

I thought about the young girl in the article I'd read earlier, and all of the oppressed women around the world. Part of my mission was to make education more accessible in places where ignorance motivates egregious action. As far as my own experiences were concerned, I knew that my higher education could not replace actually working, living, and breathing within an Islamic culture, and nothing could've prepared me for the work I was about to do in Iraq.

To help people, one must first understand their ways and their culture, through their history, but also through their underlying passions and motivations. I knew it would be important for me to gain the trust of the people I was going to meet in the coming weeks. I wanted to show by example, how individuals and societies can flourish when basic human rights are protected. My example needed to be simple, believable, and attainable.

My wandering mind jolted back into the present moment

as the small plane landed at Diyarbakir Airport, near the Iraqi border. I was immediately greeted by two non-English speaking gentlemen, Bazit and Mohammed. The men and the car matched the identification Mussafer had told me to confirm, so I knew I was with the right people.

As we drove closer to the border, I saw that there were three or four very long lanes of trucks and oil tankers heading into Iraq. Each lane must have been four to six miles long, leading up to the border. I was unable to ask what they were doing, since I didn't speak Turkish, but later I found out that they were convoys trucking oil products into Iraq. Oil from Iraq is sent to Turkey to be refined, and then trucked back into Iraq for use in gas stations and roadside container sales. Iraq has tons of oil, but no refineries. It has to do with import, export and cost. The convoys had been stopped for several months after coalition forces had taken over the country, and this was the first surge of trucks allowed to reenter Iraq since then.

As far as individuals wishing to cross the border were concerned, there was less of a wait, depending upon who was helping you. Taxis were used to shuttle people back and forth across the border. For people crossing without diplomatic representation, the delay could take up to twenty hours. Fortunately, I was accompanied by the right people, so it went pretty smoothly. Caravans of United Nations trucks and police utility vehicles were exiting Iraq at the border as I was arriving in Erbil, a heavily populated city in northern Iraq, considered at the time to be one of the more stable regions of the country.

Out of over 25 million Iraqis, over 1 million of Saddam Hussein's Ba'ath party sympathizers were still in Iraq at the time I arrived. The sympathizers clashed with those supporting the new order, causing instability and upheaval. Although the area that we were driving through was relatively secure, a feeling of

155

distrust and anxiety permeated the air.

While I was in Iraq, the country was in the process of introducing new currency, and citizens were given three months to exchange the old for the new. This was seen as a positive reform, since under Saddam's regime, any money placed in a bank was subject to theft, creating instability for those trying to gain financial profits through hard work. One northern Iraqi contractor I met told me that he had put over $1000 into a bank to support his family. Since he hadn't joined Saddam's party, the Ba'athists took half of his savings, which caused severe hardship for his family. I felt cautiously optimistic that with the fall of Saddam's regime, the people of Iraq could keep the money that they earned, but I knew it would take a long time for the government to gain the trust of its citizens after so many years of corruption. In the meantime, Iraqi citizens were just trying to survive.

Another source told me that the supporters of Saddam's party who benefited financially through their alliance were only now experiencing the poverty that the rest of the Iraqi people had been struggling with over the last forty-five years. As I listened to people's stories, I started to understand that Iraqis had no point of reference from which to define stability or democracy. The only way that peace could be established would be for the United States and the other coalition countries to lead by example. The United States would have to understand and respect the fact that the Iraqi people, though hopeful, had little trust for authority. I hoped to learn enough from this trip, and make the right contacts for World Care, in order to be able to help as many Iraqis as possible.

I noticed very little military presence during the drive through the country. We came to a stretch of road that had once been occupied by Saddam Hussein and his elite guard. Previously, it had only been accessible to the military; Iraqi civilians could not use it. Locals said it was like getting a brand new freeway, and for those who traveled frequently, it was a big deal. As we drove along this newly opened stretch of super-highway, we passed hundreds of military training sites built by Saddam, and thousands of acres scattered with abandoned bunkers and other military structures.

In the villages, women were dressed in traditional Islamic garb, with black coverings from head to toe, including their faces. As we traveled closer to town, their clothes were less constricting. Although their bodies remained covered from head to toe, they no longer wore headdresses.

We arrived at the hotel in Erbil, Iraq at 8:30 p.m. It was humid, cloudy and rainy, and I was thankful that the ride was finally over. I was exhausted. My room was modest, with two single beds, a refrigerator, a bathroom with a western style toilet, a table and two chairs, a television with cable, local phone, lights, and clean sheets. A man passed me in the hall as I was entering my room. He whispered "if you value anything, take it with you." "What?" You heard me, have a good sleep."

CHAPTER TWENTY-ONE

Face to Face with Tragedy

On my first full day in Iraq, I was scheduled to meet with Counterpart and International Blue Crescent, the two main NGO's (nongovernmental organizations) that World Care would be collaborating with for our Middle East projects. It was a Friday morning, which, like our Sunday in the United States, is a day of rest. I woke up around 9:00 a.m. and helped myself to the buffet breakfast included in the cost of the room.

The restaurant was filled with a variety of workers. I became highly conscious of the fact that I had seen only one other woman in the past hour. The men sat around watching a program on the big screen TV in the lobby. For the first time, Iraqis were able to watch international networks like BBC, MTV and CNN. Everything was subtitled in Arabic. Prior to the fall of Saddam's regime, the only network allowed to broadcast had been Al Jazeera, which showed only propaganda and news controlled by Saddam. I was hopeful that the introduction of international cable television, cell phones, and the Internet, would provide tools that could bring a different perspective to the once isolated country.

Iraqi governmental employees had earned only about three or four dollars per month under Saddam Hussein, and now the United States was paying $120 to $130 per month for the same work. The United States was beginning to offer new social services to Iraqi citizens as well. To jump start the economy, people who were not currently employed but who had degrees were given $60 to $70 per month to live on until they could find jobs. Iraq was beginning to be a country moving forward with entrepreneurial thinking. I observed and met people who embraced the change.

I spent the day addressing issues faced by local NGO's that were participating in northern Kurdistan, central, and southern Iraq. Kurdish history was a hot topic in the conversations concerning problems within Iraqi culture. In the 1970's the ruling Ba'ath party began a push to clear out large groups of Kurds from their homes and businesses in what the United Nations and international community later recognized as ethnic cleansing.

Tragically, thousands of Kurds were murdered or displaced. Many of those displaced moved into central and southern Iraq. Survivors were forced to relocate to government-controlled areas similar to the Nazi concentration camps during World War II. In 2003, the Kurds were still considered and treated as an underclass population.

This "Arabization" was an attempt to overturn the Kurdish majorities in provinces rich with oil. People spoke of Kurds being driven out of the northern city of Kirkuk because of their refusal to assimilate. The Iraqi government restricted Kurds from purchasing homes unless they were willing to become Arab. Kurdish gravestones were rubbed out and replaced with Arabic names. During the years 1986 and 1987, Saddam Hussein destroyed approximately 4,000 Kurdish villages.

My confidence waned as to whether the US invasion of Iraq was a wise move, but I felt hopeful that it would bring much needed progress to the region, especially in the area of human rights. There was so much to be done that any small amount of progress made a huge impact. For instance, when I arrived, even the more advanced parts of the country had no postal system.

There was no form of legal representation or individual protection whatsoever. While I was sitting in a car at an intersection controlled by a military officer with a semi-automatic weapon, two teenagers attempted to drive through on their motorbikes. The officer stopped one of the teens, grabbed his collar, and slapped him in the face. Then he cocked his weapon to stop the other teen. I couldn't imagine meter-maids or traffic cops getting away with that in the United States, or any other place for that matter where people have basic civil rights.

Minor infractions such as traffic violations were all handled in similar disproportionately violent ways because there was no system of law in place. That translated into no ticket writing, no probation officers, and no community service. In many instances, unfair, violent justice was carried out immediately by an officer who was essentially a government sanctioned bully. There were no banking systems, no credit cards, no Laundromats, no social services, no emergency healthcare system, no clinics for women— the list went on and on. There was a jail however, located in the basement of a hospital, and a long term prison housing over 5,000 inmates.

The next day I woke up early, mistakenly thinking that I was late for a 6:00 a.m. pick-up. It was daylight savings but the clocks hadn't been changed. Once I realized I had extra time, I was able to relax and have a leisurely breakfast. A gentleman named Kamoran from a Turkmani NGO drove me to Kirkuk, a city about 75 miles north of Erbil that had been heavily occupied by the Ba'ath Party, to visit three of the major projects we would be working on.

Our first stop was a hospital that had been a prison and a torture facility used by Saddam Hussein's henchmen. Hooks from which people had been hung, and torture bars, were still in place. The bloodstained floors and walls were a horrifying reminder of Saddam's methods. Thousands of people died in such facilities in atrocious ways. Since Saddam had been ousted, the buildings had been abandoned and then taken over by local NGOs to build schools and clinics. The organization that World Care had been collaborating with had acquired two of these facilities. Allowing organizations to recycle the former "crimes against humanity buildings" into useful places where children's and women's centers could flourish was an important move, both practically and symbolically.

U.S. troops were everywhere. Everyone had weapons—semi-automatics, pistols, machetes, even grenades. Saddam had yet to be found. When we arrived at the second building we were visiting, we saw an AmeriCare sign out front. This building was situated behind a ten-story building used for intelligence that had been bombed earlier in the year. Scores of recruited child soldiers had been trained here, and it had also been used as a weapons cache. Random shots rang out as we left the building and I quickly moved toward the car. My guide pulled out his pistol and others took cover. Fortunately, no one was hurt, but the gunman was never identified. We drove to our next meeting cautiously after that incident. My schedule was modified as a safety precaution. We traveled mostly by random taxis from then on so that we wouldn't draw attention to ourselves.

We headed back to Erbil after our final meeting. On the way, I got out of the car to videotape some of the oil fields that ran for over a hundred miles. Some were on fire. The causes of the fires were unknown, although possibilities included spontaneous combustion. One of the passengers I was traveling with, Muem, joked that you could dig a hole just twelve inches deep anywhere in Iraq, and start a fire for a cookout. We passed many abandoned training camps that had been previously occupied by Saddam's military. There were dozens of old tanks being stripped down and sold to Turkey or Jordan for salvage profit. We also passed a number of beautiful, castle-like buildings, resting in grassy fields. Immediately, I recognized potential farmland for future agricultural growth. Unfortunately, the buildings and adjacent fields were filled with landmines. Many squatters sought refuge here anyway, including women and children.

When we returned to Erbil that evening, I met with Gelewash, the director of operations in Kurdistan, Iraq. We'd been in contact for many months, so it was a pleasure to finally meet her in person. She was petite, only about 5'2", with dark hair and a warm smile. We dove into conversation about our project, logistics, expectations, shipments, and hotel accommodations for the numerous volunteers. For five hours we went through the preliminaries, and chatted about morals, philosophy, world events, passions, and goals. Her driver, bodyguard, and the owner of the hotel, joined our animated and inspiring conversation.

Much of our work hinged upon how we were going to ship and distribute the education and humanitarian supplies, and ensuring that they arrived at the correct destinations. The biggest challenge that humanitarian aid organizations face regarding international projects is keeping track of shipments and holding people accountable for the distribution of supplies. While mailing a box of books or hiring a moving company is simple and routine in most developed countries, getting supplies to and from Iraq was a logistical nightmare. Fortunately, World Care and other NGOs found ways to work together to accomplish distribution goals.

As disturbing as the bloodstained prison-turned-hospital was, nothing could have prepared me for visits to the clinics where children and elderly people were being cared for after having been harmed by the experiments of the notorious doctor, "Chemical Ali," who had concocted chemical weaponry for Saddam.   Inside the first clinic, children lined the hallways on stretchers with IV's piercing their delicate limbs.   One little boy no more than four years old lay in bed with his forearms bandaged. I asked the doctor what had happened to this child as I stroked his little head. The doctor told me that the boy's hands were blown off and that he had been blinded by a bomb deliberately placed in a toy to maim children. The bombs were not intended to kill the children, but to harm them enough so they would always be reminded of their inferiority as they grew up. "The lucky ones died, the doctor said sadly."

I thought to myself, this is how hatred is perpetuated for generations to come.

The conditions of the people I met and the stories I heard were unbelievably tragic.   There were several women who had been brutally raped and were now lying in catatonic states in beds at the end of the hallway. I heard of one woman, not much younger than I, who had died after being strangled by a family member for speaking her mind. Rows of people with amputations caused by landmines sat in chairs awaiting care. Hospital supplies were scarce and out of date. Basic supplies like gauze and tape were nowhere to be found. My heart broke as I saw children occupying endlessly crowded rooms and hallways.

There was no justification for these crimes against humanity. Most of the 25 million Iraqis simply wanted to go to school, work and raise their families, just like the rest of us. The people who committed these crimes were not human. I wondered what kind of person it took to think, "Today I'm going to hurt children so that one day I will be rewarded with many virgin women in heaven." This was not a religious war, nor an ethnic war; this was a war between good and evil.

The painful images of the injured children were seared into my memory. At the conclusion of my assessment, I had a long list of supplies that urgently needed to be shipped. I left the clinic with absolute certainty that the work of non-profit organizations was a necessity. I was thankful that I had followed my intuition in creating World Care. It was the only thing to do at the time, but I recognized then that it was the right thing to do, too.

My spirits lifted after we left the clinic and met with family members of those with whom I was collaborating. The ladies conferred with each another and decided that it was time to play "dress up Lisa," since there was a party the following Thursday evening. Apparently, I needed an Iraqi makeover.

Kemoran's wife pulled a beautiful blue toque from her wardrobe. It was an elaborate outfit, comprised of six pieces, which was standard fashion. Then out came the accessories-- ornate gold bracelets and necklaces. I couldn't believe the amount of gold these women wore. When asked why, they explained that it was their form of savings because there was no banking system. Instead of depositing money into a checking or savings account, they bought gold and wore it. Once they acquired a lot of gold, they could sell it to local merchants to buy homes, or anything else they needed. The women asked me if people in the U.S. wore much gold. I explained that gold was popular, but not the 22 carat variety that they adorn themselves with in Iraq.

We concluded the evening with tea and fresh fruit. It was a light finish to a heavy day. The entire family of eight piled into the car to escort me back to the hotel. They were so welcoming and hospitable and I was very appreciative. So full of dissonance from morning to night, I wonder what lie ahead for the next day.

CHAPTER TWENTY-TWO

The Long Road to Baghdad

I woke up the next day after sleeping for fifteen hours straight. I'd missed breakfast, but at lunch I struck up a conversation with an American named John, a retired military officer who worked for an independent contractor with security and Special Forces. John was overseeing and protecting the technical personnel who were setting up satellite television across Iraq. He'd been in Iraq for two months, since early August. Several of his colleagues quickly joined our conversation. They all shared similar commando, body-builder, Special Forces type builds. I instantly felt very safe among them.

John explained that civilians were being trained in Louisiana for anti-terrorist tactics, and being sent to the Middle East. I felt reassured when he told me that Erbil, where I was staying, was the safest and nicest place in Iraq, other than the mountain region of the northern border, which had adobe-like homes nestled in the outcroppings of high peaks. From John's description, I imagined it looked like New Mexico.

Later that day I was scheduled to attended a meeting in Mosul with military personnel. Security was very high because of the U.S. occupation and the potential for extremist groups to act out violently against them.   On our way, we passed a site where two car-bombings had taken place earlier in the day, claiming the lives of four people.   Despite added security measures, civilians were still being killed every week.

I passed through security on the base rather quickly, since my entry had been approved ahead of time.   A representative from another international aid organization accompanied me to work out the details of storage and distribution of the aid supplies World Care was preparing to send over.   The base was under construction, and everyone including the construction workers, was dressed in battle gear. I guess I missed the memo.

When we arrived at the office, the conversation immediately moved to assessment of needs for our project. We met with Lt. Colonel Jackie Russell, who was in charge of roughly eight hundred personnel.   She had the ability to receive and distribute supplies to many regions in Iraq, and I was thrilled that she had extended her support to World Care and our counterpart. With the help of the military, we could expand our projects and reach more people.

Lt. Russell showed me around the base which was literally a small city complete with many American amenities.   There was a 24/7 Internet café, a dance hall, restaurants, and a juice bar. Instructional video tapes, movie DVDs, and music were available. The troops also had the opportunity to participate in humanitarian aid projects, which included helping children in four schools and starting an Iraqi girls' basketball team. The Lt. Colonel told me that morale was being maintained although the announcement that these troops would be in Iraq until March 2004 hit their spirits hard.

To avoid bandits who were targeting SUVs and other expensive vehicles with increased frequency, I decided to travel to Baghdad by taxi the following day. We departed just as the sun was rising, illuminating wide open spaces and the occasional warning signs for landmines. Fortunately, our journey was uneventful. Low mountains outlined the horizon in beautiful shades of red, yellow, and pink. The smell of gasoline permeated the air. Air pollution was at an all-time high. As the sun rose higher, a brown haze veiled the landscape. We were taking the long road to Baghdad just south of the Kurdish regions where nomads took up refuge in abandoned military bunkers and prison fortresses once occupied by Saddam.

The road had no center lines, no traffic signs, and no speed limits. There were BMWs passing donkey carts, truly a sight to behold. People sold fruit along the highway and garbage was burning in the streets as cars zoomed crazily by. A little bit of everything was happening all at once. Compared to the order that was commonplace in America, the experience of traveling in Iraq was absolute chaos. I learned the true art and paid skill of passing other vehicles in Iraq. Taxi drivers careen into oncoming traffic at 90 to 100 miles per hour, then cut back only when they can see the hairs growing out of the oncoming driver's ear. One wrong move and we were all dead, I thought, tightly clutching my seatbelt, as if it would help. What was the damn rush?

As we drove past Kirkuk, we witnessed more burning oil wells and gas refineries. The emptiness gave way to electrical lines as far as the eye could see. Abandoned grain silos lined the roads, and there were many half-built structures. Every guard post that we passed was vandalized with defaced portraits of Saddam. Herds of goats, sheep, and lamb grazed along the side of the road. After three and a half hair-raising hours, thankfully we reached Baghdad.

The city was weathered with age and had seen terrible abuse. Buildings were cracked and all the paint was faded, broken concrete sidewalks lined streets filled with garbage. Curbs had been broken by tanks running over them. The air was thick with smog and packed with cars, and there was no air-conditioning anywhere. It was like inhaling an exhaust pipe. I held my breath until it was no longer an option. Then I sucked in the polluted air and wondered if not breathing would've kept me alive longer.

We passed by a large university in Baghdad where students and U.S. military were gathered. Iraqis were lining up to receive the compensation promised by the U.S. government: $10 for those who had completed primary school, $20 for high school, and $60 for college graduates with no job. It was an attempt to start a social support system, a stimulus plan for Iraq.

My colleague, Karmaron, with whom I'd traveled to Baghdad, secured a meeting with the local County Director, Thomas Benton, in hopes of shedding some light on the NGO situation. It was apparent that after the U.N. was bombed most of the international NGO's quickly deserted the country, since many of the offices we visited had been closed and abandoned. It was important, as part of the needs assessment, that I have an understanding of how much the local support would be willing to stick it out. The office was bare. There were no computers, no telephones, no books, just lighting and basic furniture. Thomas told us that most people working with NGOs had to be undercover because of the deep hatred for Americans among the Iraqi youth. He explained that it was impossible to distinguish friends from foes.

After the meeting, we drove further into the city. Demonstrations and rallies were being held, at which no cameras were allowed by military forces. Months after the United States' initial invasion, there was still a lot of unrest, more so in southern Iraq. The city was packed with people, business activity, and students. The U.S. military was highly visible, standing guard with fully loaded automatic machine guns. Armored bank vehicles lined the entrance to the University where another delivery of money for students was being made.

It was clear that much work would be needed to put the city back together. Everyone in Iraq referred to time there as either pre- or post-1991, the year that the United States first placed sanctions and embargos on Iraq for bombing Kuwait. Prior to that, Saddam was demanding and receiving money from Kuwait for "protecting" them as a neighboring country. After the Iran/Iraq war of 1988, things changed drastically for the people of Kuwait, and they refused to continue paying Saddam, claiming they were not being protected at all.

Angered by Kuwait's decision, Saddam bombed and invaded them. The United States came in to support Kuwait and fight off Saddam. Since Iraq had received huge amounts of funding from the United States before bombing Kuwait, the economic sanctions the US put on Iraq literally stopped the country in its tracks. Even though Iraq was one of the richest countries when it came to natural resources, the wealth was so unevenly distributed that the country simultaneously had one of the world's highest poverty rates. In addition to poverty, crimes against humanity, corruption, and lack of sovereignty had always been a way of life.

Before me I saw a nation of people who were trying to earn a living and make lives for themselves. I sensed their pain and resentment for all they had endured over the years. I hoped that the suffering of their past would not return again. I prayed that the country could move on and prosper. On the drive back to Erbil, we stopped to eat at a roadside restaurant. When we walked in, I saw only men. As soon as the waiter saw me, he quickly shuffled our group upstairs to the "family area" for men *and* women. At that moment, I was fully reminded that Iraq had far deeper problems than the immediate violence at hand. It was entrenched in the culture that women were considered second-class citizens to their male counterparts, and regardless of our humanitarian efforts, this was not going to change anytime soon.

The next few days in Iraq became a blur; they were so full and very long. I spent the majority of my time interviewing individuals about their experiences meeting with government officials and NGOs, and reviewing contracts and requests for supplies. Several more organizations joined World Care's collaborative mission. Funding for our projects remained an issue, but as the news poured in that the U.S. House of Representatives had approved $87 billion in support for Iraq and Afghanistan, we were optimistic about our prospects for funding. If there was ever a country that would be able to pay back a debt, it would be Iraq. Most people I spoke with were happy to have Saddam gone. Among the civilians in Iraq there was a general feeling that this was the dawning of a new beginning for them. The country abounded with natural resources, and the opportunity for a new beginning seemed promising. And yet, despite the potential and longings for change, the road to peace and prosperity for the Iraqi people would prove to be a long and arduous one.

I'd been staying in the hotel for over a week, and noticed that gradually the hospitality had improved. Perhaps I had some seniority over the shorter staying guests, because on that particular morning, I was granted a window seat at breakfast. Heading through the lobby on my way back to my room, I encountered a friendly American man in a flak jacket who struck up a conversation with me. He wondered aloud if the hotel served breakfast, so with my newfound guest status, I confidently escorted him to the restaurant. I gladly joined him and two of his friends for coffee at his request.

Our conversation thickened from chit-chat to questions about resources on the ground. It turned out that two of the three, whom I'll call Tom and Dave, were responsible for protecting the life of the third man, named Sam. Sam was in the banking industry, and was responsible for securing the banks in Iraq and replacing old money with the new. Tom and Dave were both Special Forces and SEAL trained. They invited me to tag along with them for the day, and ever interested in seeing and learning more, I accepted.

We piled into two SUVs and drove away from the hotel. I had no idea where we were headed, somewhere dangerous I had to assume, since Tom and Dave packed enough weapons for a small army. We drove to a secure military fortress outside of Erbil, near the Iran border. It had CIA written all over it. Inside was a five-star resort hotel, complete with a gym. CIA officials and intelligence people were everywhere. Tom and Dave checked us in and we looked around. Mostly, the men shared war stories. I imagined them retired someday, sitting in a bar, reminiscing about their more exciting adventures.

I enjoyed getting to know Tom and Dave. Tom was twice divorced with three kids, and he came from a military family. Like me, he was a twin, but his sibling had not lived. Tom, in turn, had twin boys with his second wife. He had enjoyed a remarkable career, traveling all over the world, protecting "assets." His luck with women, however, ran a bit short. Dave was a 6'5" southern boy who loved horses and was dedicated to his job. For fun, he enjoyed scuba diving with sharks, and he called his parents often to check in. Both men had been ambushed several times since being in Iraq. Before sundown, they drove me back to my hotel. I said goodbye and hoped that they would get home safely to their families.

On my last full day in Iraq, I traveled to Kirkuk to distribute

171

school supplies to the local students and NGOs supporting them. By the time we arrived in Kirkuk, the temperature had risen above ninety degrees. The warehouse was hot and claustrophobic, packed with teachers eager to receive the last portion of the supplies that we had shipped in.

I had the opportunity to interview a few of the teachers. One voiced her opinion about how important it was to have removed Saddam. She told me that he had impoverished the education system and its employees during his reign and that only Ba'ath supporters made money. "We are very happy this has happened. He was a very bad man," she told me.

We went from the warehouse to the schools, delivering school boxes with supplies and new desks. The children greeted us by singing songs, clapping their hands, and whistling cheerfully. They were excited to receive the gifts for their schools. I was glad to help, but this was only the tip of the iceberg. There was still so much more needed to improve their quality of education and life.

Contrasting with our lively visits to the schools, we made a much more somber stop at a refugee camp for Kurds who had been displaced from their homes. An old jail had been converted into temporary homes for hundreds of people. It was hard for me to imagine seeking refuge in a place like this. Ten people were crammed into rooms of about one hundred square feet, and there were no bathrooms. The children did not attend school. The people spent most of their time in the yard, making the best of their desperate situation.

I saw one woman making bread, another washing, and another attending to some children. As soon as they realized my purpose, they began to tell me what they needed. Their excitement was infectious. Many of the women were widowed because Saddam had killed their husbands for not joining his Ba'ath party. The women wanted to earn money but there weren't any jobs available to Kurds mainly because the economy had collapsed. This same story was told to me by countless women during my time in Iraq.

Everywhere we went there were not only soldiers, but business owners packing machine guns, hand guns, and semi-automatic rifles. The new Iraqi military was forming while I was there, and it was easy to tell the seasoned soldiers from the new ones. The new members stood proud and alert, and they inspected cars very thoroughly. The experienced guards sat around complacently and moved us on with a wave of the hand. My personal experience in the military in the early eighties made it easier for me to feel relatively comfortable in this environment, since I was already familiar with military protocol. I imagine that people without any military experience would have a much more difficult time remaining calm in such a tense environment.

Back in Erbil I met up with my new friends from another NGO at a local eatery, and we had a wonderful last meal together. They expressed how grateful they were for World Care's involvement with their humanitarian efforts. Our last stop before heading to a farewell party that evening was at a local community center where the people were building facilities for children to learn how to work on computers. The party was fun and it was an uplifting end to a rollercoaster trip.

I made some wonderful new friends during the short time I had been in Iraq and I was going to miss them. Everyone I'd worked with was gracious, polite, fun, and very accommodating. I had genuine respect for their optimism and fortitude to rebuild. I felt lucky to have met them all.

The next morning I awoke at "zero-dark-thirty a.m.", military slang for "in the middle of the night," to pack my bags. They were so stuffed that they barely closed. I felt like a cliché -an American returning home from a trip abroad with more than

I came with. I scanned the room that I had called home for the past ten days to make sure I hadn't missed packing anything. I felt very safe there and was surprised to find that I was a little sad about leaving. I went downstairs, paid the balance for my room and had my final breakfast of a boiled egg, yogurt, fruit and chai. I bumped into Tom and Dave, the guys from the "unknown agency" who had performed a very subtle interrogation on me just days before in the restaurant. We had one final chat before my departure. We exchanged contact information, and they reminded me that if I ever needed protection, they were my men. I was glad that I'd run into them again because regardless of who they are or where they come from, it's always important to have friends where enemies linger.

Kamaran arrived at the hotel and collected my bags for the long drive back to Diyarbakir, Turkey. We left promptly at 9:00 a.m. and arrived at the border by noon. Another gentleman met us at the border and loaded my belongings into his car. He took my passport, completed my border processing in less than thirty minutes, and we were off for a five hour drive toward Istanbul. This time, there were center lines on the road, so I felt much more relaxed than I had on the trip to Iraq.

We drove through a part of Turkey that was beautiful and reminded me of home in Arizona. There was desert, farmland, and earth-colored adobe houses. I chatted with the driver in expressive hand gestures since we didn't speak each other's language. As usual, there was no air-conditioning in the car, but the outside air was clean and mild. I enjoyed the breeze coming in through the open windows. With my hair flying every which way, I was a sight to see, but at that point, vanity was the last thing on my mind.

The driver took me to a lovely hotel about two hours outside of Istanbul, housed inside an ancient castle that was over

6,000 years old. A woman greeted me in English and told me that dinner would be served whenever I was hungry. A bellboy brought my heavy bags up twelve steep, stone-cut stairs to the second floor. The door opening to my room was only five feet tall. I felt like Alice in Wonderland entering my room for the night. The room had two single beds and a large window overlooking a negative edge pool. The place reminded me of the convent in Chile, only better, because I had my own bathroom.

I awoke the next morning not having slept as restfully as I had hoped in such a tranquil environment. I dressed and went downstairs for breakfast. The early morning air was cool and damp. I tried to imagine what it would have been like to live in the castle 6,000 years ago, before Christ, Mohammed, and Buddha. The steep stairs and tiny doors didn't match up in my imagination. Did midgets with long legs live here back then, or better, mountain goats? I asked the proprietors why the doors were so small, envisioning elves occupying the place, but they told me that they had been designed purposely to cause a person to bow upon entry into the room.

I arrived at the local airport ten minutes before it opened. My only mission for the day was to snag a standby seat on a flight from London to the United States that evening. I already had my flight to Istanbul, and then on to London, so I figured I had a good shot.

CHAPTER TWENTY-THREE

Food for Oil Fiasco

Shortly after arriving home from Iraq and completing the assessment, I was off on another humanitarian request for a needs assessment, this time to Georgia, Russia to check on supplies and equipment we had sent. On the day I was traveling, the State Department issued a travelers' warning: "Attention all travelers. Be advised that there are potential terrorist activities in the following countries in the Middle East, Europe, and Africa…" I started to wonder if there was any place left on earth that didn't come with a travelers' warning. I was also attending a ceremony in honor of the medical humanitarian aid we provided.

This particular delegation included non-governmental and non-religious organizations representing Turkey, the Kurds, and the United States. For many years, Muslim fundamentalist groups like the Taliban had oppressed women and children in many parts of the Middle East. I hoped that this small peace-keeping initiative would set in motion the liberation of women and children by providing education, healthcare, and human rights--basic needs which they had been deprived of for so long.

I traveled to Georgia from Tucson via Chicago and

176

London. The entire trip, as scheduled, was supposed to take twenty-four hours. I arrived first in Chicago where I was met with freezing temperatures, snow, a delay of six hours and a surprise! My sister Pam and my father had come to meet me. It was Groundhog's Day, which was also Pam's birthday, and they came to the airport to take me to lunch. I felt so happy to see them, and was comforted to have them see me off on what was going to be an adventure in Russia.

After lunch, they walked me back to the security checkpoint where I passed through to meet my flight to London. I saw gray skies and heavy snow from the windows in my terminal. Bundled up airline employees were de-icing planes and reviewing the board for cancellations. I had a feeling this was going to be a never-ending day. While I waited for my flight, my cell phone rang. It was my friend Brian in Washington, who had been working on the Iraqi projects with me. He told me that he had just received word that the containers of humanitarian aid supplies that World Care had sent had arrived in Iraq, and would be delivered to the warehouse after customs cleared the paperwork. That was good news.

"Also, there has been a change in plans," he informed me. "I can't go into details, but we've had an incident in Tbilisi, Georgia. You'll be meeting a new country director upon your arrival. I'll email you the information. You can pick it up at Heathrow Airport in London. In the meantime, have a safe trip."

That was unexpected. "Wait, what happened to Shentroviko?" I asked. Shentroviko was the gentleman in Georgia with whom I'd been corresponding, and had planned to work with upon arrival.

"I can't go into it right now," Brian replied, "but they are expecting you in twenty-four hours." The phone went dead.

177

Finally, I was able to board my delayed airplane. I was bumped to first class, so I couldn't complain about the delay. I settled into my seat and pulled out my agenda for the next couple of weeks. I reviewed the plans, making mental notes of my alternatives since, according to Brian, I could no longer stick with Plan A. I looked through the notes and pictures in my dream book, to make sure I hadn't missed any symbols or events to look out for on my journey. Nothing jumped out at me. After dinner and two Tylenol PMs, I drifted off to sleep, pondering the unique chain of events that had led me to this point in my life. I didn't wake until morning, when the plane landed in London.

I was scheduled for an overnight layover in London, but since I felt rested from my first class snooze, I decided to try to get on an earlier flight to Istanbul where I could connect to my flight to Georgia a bit earlier. I got lucky and several hours later, I was on a flight to my favorite Turkish city. I still had no word yet on what was happening with the change of people and plans in Georgia. I didn't have time to call Brian in Washington before heading to the gate.

I arrived in Istanbul early in the evening, and immediately called my contact and friend Mussafer to let him know that I'd arrived early. He was in Kabul, Afghanistan, and would be returning to Istanbul the following morning. We agreed that we would meet at noon the following day to chat about our plans in Georgia. I spent the night in a clean, comfortable, and modest hotel near the airport and gave myself a pat on the back because had I spent the night in London, it would have cost me twice as much.

Georgia, once part of the former Soviet Union, had serious concerns with regional stability. Shevardnadze, a former Soviet high official, had brought some stability but there were still many challenges in the volatile region. Mikhail Shakashvili, the new president-elect of the Republic of Georgia, had his hands full with the problems faced by the newly independent country. Georgia's stability, or lack thereof, has historically had regional and international significance because it is the main thoroughfare of major export pipelines of oil and gas. Also, the United States occupied parts of the country for its operations in Iraq, Afghanistan, and other Middle Eastern countries.

The United States had recently committed to supplying Georgia with humanitarian aid for an unlimited amount of time. Since 1991, Georgia had already received over $1.2 billion in aid assistance from the United States. In addition to the humanitarian funding, the United States introduced the Georgian Train and Equipment Program (GTEP) in April 2002, in order to enable Tblisi, Georgia to protect and secure its borders in support of the war against terrorism. Tblisi, Georgia is located only 40 kilometers from the Chechnya, a region known for terrorist activity outside of Georgian jurisdiction.

Relations between Georgia and the Russian Kremlin had been strained ever since the new president-elect of Georgia had taken office. He had recently proposed sending the Russian military back to their homeland, an action that would place him in grave danger. Terrorism was a large concern, and the president's assassination by the Russian military seemed almost inevitable.

According to sources in Georgia, there were major concerns that Afghani refugees had moved through Pakistan to other countries, and were organizing massive attacks to take place in the United States and other allied countries. In Afghanistan, there was good reason to fear that Pakistani officials had been supporting Al Qaeda, and that even United Nations workers could be involved in giving food to the groups in exchange for safety: Al Qaeda not bombing the aid camps. It was hard to know who to believe. Many local tribes in and around Kabul were being paid off not to terrorize the international peacekeeping workers. These people were influenced by money, and played both sides, trading drugs and arms to support terrorist activities.

I flew to Georgia that evening, arriving in the middle of the night. Sergey Khomehenko, our counterpart director, met me there. He had been in the Soviet military and now lived in Kiev, Ukraine, serving in Counterpart's emergency aid division. It was a short ride to the quaint hotel where we were staying, and after a short briefing and a few hours of sleep, we were off to tour area facilities.

The itinerary was packed on that first day. We visited the Heart and Vessel hospital before moving on to the Labor and Delivery Hospital, then a children's school, followed by a meeting with the U.S. Ambassador to Georgia, Richard Miles. The long day ended in a meeting with Kent Larson, the liaison in charge of social transition and development for United States Agency of Independent Development (USAID).

The next day, I had a meeting with the non-profit medical humanitarian organization, Hippocrates, a Greek organization headquartered in Chicago with projects in Ukraine, Georgia, and Armenia. They were collaborating with Counterpart and had recently begun accepting supplies from World Care to meet the needs in and around Chechnya and Tbilisi.

After that meeting, I sat down with USAID to review the current projects and determine how the political situation might affect our progress. Later that afternoon, I met with the Finance Ministry in order to understand how funding was being directed toward education in general, and specifically toward qualified health professionals. It was clear to me that a lot of work needed to be done as far as accountability and distribution were concerned.

Humanitarian efforts were already underway in Georgia although the economy was broken and eighty percent of the population was unemployed. People lined up at free clinics to see doctors, and so the humanitarian aid money had been well spent. Despite a desperate need for continued humanitarian aid, supply shipments were too often blocked by officers who claimed that the aid workers were taking patients away from paid clinics, thereby interfering with the economy. The new president had vowed to end this widespread corruption and to build a stronger economy. My needs assessment for the area was fairly straightforward. Over thirty percent of the patients at the hospitals and clinics had major heart problems, so World Care's donation of a cardiac angiography suite would be widely used and greatly appreciated.

That evening, I allowed myself to unwind over a delicious meal of traditional Georgian food, which included fresh spinach, fish, and wonderful cheese dishes. The Georgian culture prides itself on hospitality and I was grateful to be on the receiving end of their warmth.

I finally learned why I was met by Sergey Khomehenko instead of by Shentroviko, the original person from Counterpart with whom I'd been collaborating before my trip. Khomehenko had taken over as Regional Director for Counterpart Georgia. He had moved to Georgia from Kiev after Shentroviko had abruptly changed positions several months earlier. Apparently, the former director had been threatened to the point where bullets were fired at his office, which led to his relocation. Shentroviko, a former Soviet military police officer, had past experience working in humanitarian aid while in the service. After he retired from the military, he began working with an international NGO, starting out as a volunteer and eventually moving his way up in the organization. He spoke fluent Russian, Georgian, English, and Ukranian, often chatting with field workers, school principals, healthcare workers, and science professors. I had learned a lot about the current situation from him.

A year earlier, a container of vegetable oil had bee sent to Georgia as part of a program called "Food for Oil." Under this program, oil was supposed to be brought into the country and sold as a commodity on the open market. In return, schools would get free vegetable oil, an expensive item in Georgia. When the shipment arrived, the canisters were distributed to a group of schools through their directors. According to sources, the oil never reached the children. The directors sold the oil and either pocketed the money or gave it to an unknown source. A former congressman from Arizona who had at one point joined one of the aid organizations and was later fired, was responsible for this corrupt program. He now lives in the Ukraine with his new wife. He tried to secure employment with USAID but was turned down. Even worse, there is speculation that the U.S. government was involved with this person and his Food for Oil program, but this is unconfirmed. At the time, efforts were still underway to identify those involved. More investigations were needed to look into dealings with contacts on the Senate Congressional Committee.

Upon hearing this story, I recalled a conversation I'd had several days earlier with Richard Miles, the US Ambassador to Georgia. He had explained that most of the country's money problems were rooted in governmental corruption. Although there were still difficulties with distribution of money and supplies to intended recipients, he remained conservatively optimistic. It was my understanding that Richard Miles played a major role in helping the new Georgian president come to power. Apparently B.P. Oil Company was having no trouble getting $3 billion worth of funding for the oil pipelines to the right people. I understood the region's priorities. While billions of dollars were being pumped into the oil industry, government workers, police, doctors and teachers had not been paid for months, yet still dutifully performed their jobs. None of their buildings had any heat, and electricity was rationed at six hours per day. Desperate people resort to desperate measures: with eighty percent of the population unemployed, this was a major reason for much of the corruption.

I left feeling sad about the state of the region and the scale of corruption that would have to be surmounted for the country to prosper. I reminded myself that I couldn't carry that entire burden on my shoulders. World Care and other non-profit NGOs were doing everything we could. My experience in Georgia reiterated Brother Leo's warnings about corruption just as my Iraq experience had, and how important it was for World Care to work in collaboration with, but independently from, government and religious organizations.

Another dream came in the night; there was a huge storm, I was holding a baby outside a large brick school. I was in an old brick school. Lots of volunteers were around with many children. I ran down the long hall. We had lots of supplies and pallets around. Storms were outside with rain and tornadoes. Then I had a large baby in my arms. A voice sounded "You will be safe here."

I woke up, took a deep breath and hoped this dream would come to fruition.

CHAPTER TWENTY-FOUR

Tsunami

New Headquarters

I returned from my trip to Georgia to business as usual in Tucson. In 2004 I continued to work on several projects, both locally and abroad as World Care continued to experience tremendous growth and recognition. On my Birthday, August 29, 2004, Tucson's Mayor Bob Walkup signed a proclamation declaring that day to be "World Care Day" in the city of Tucson, praising our organization and its many volunteers for the programs that were helping people locally and around the world. Just a few years earlier, I would never have believed a day like this would come and that it would be on my birthday. I was truly honored.

World Care had been so successful at collecting donations that we were outgrowing our facility. Even after the distribution of school supplies in our annual Tools for Schools program, we were running out of space for the millions of pounds of supplies we had to manage. I had read an article in the local paper about an elementary school that was going to have to close as it was in the flight path of Davis Monthan Air Force Base. Several months later, Pam, in Operations, reminded me about the closure.

I waited a few days before contacting Tucson Unified School District to inquire about what the building would be used for, and if there was any possibility that the school district would consider granting World Care use of the facility. I told them that as our operations continued to expand, we could use a more permanent home that would have the space for our growing supplies and volunteers. The soon-to-be-former elementary school would be perfect.

After several phone calls, I connected with the person in charge of managing the process of finding an occupant for the building. I told him everything about World Care. He kindly took down my information and offered to contact me if he needed anything else. I offered to send him some brochures about World Care, and he gladly gave me his address to do so. I hadn't even seen the school yet, and I knew that we didn't have the money to purchase the building, and yet I had a strong feeling that we were meant to occupy it. I didn't hear back from the school district for a long time, but as I waited patiently, I continually envisioned our organization in that new home.

I stayed focused on our current projects and continued to publicize our organization. Then, on December 26, 2004, the day after Christmas, disaster struck. In South Asia, a tsunami of record size killed over 200,000 people and left millions displaced. The losses were so great that for a brief time everyone in the world laid down their differences and helped in the relief efforts. Each day the death toll rose. World Care went into emergency mode within hours of the news reaching the United States. We had the largest volunteer and donation response we had ever seen.

Sri Lanka

In January of 2005, I traveled to Sri Lanka to meet with other NGOs to assess the damage and determine how each organization could contribute. By the time I arrived there, World Care had already collaborated with five other U.S. entities to streamline the process of the mass shipments of supplies to the area.

I met with colleagues from other agencies assembled in a large briefing room for aid workers. We were triaged according to our specialty – those who specialized in medicine or forensics were given the task of helping identify the bodies that were still being found along the devastated coastline. Because the government and independent communities had buried many of the bodies just days after the event, there were large areas of possible water contamination. Thousands of corpses had yet to be identified. Since I had a background in forensics, I was sent on the identification mission.

I was teamed with several doctors and healthcare workers. As we approached our first village, the smell of dead bodies and rotting flesh permeated the hot, humid air, and I could hear cries of despair. It had been over a week since the giant wave had destroyed the coastline, and the body count was continuing to rise. We stopped and I sat in the truck and waited for instructions about how to proceed. The devastation was overwhelming.

A Sri Lankan man with a beautiful face approached us. He thanked us for coming and showed us what was left of his village. Beyond the village was a bay about seven acres in size that was full of massive amounts of debris and bodies. Our job that morning was to wade through the thick, muddy water and place flags where there might be bodies so that local construction workers and other villagers could pull the bodies out once we had located them. There were about forty of us working the shallow water wearing hip waders and carrying flags. It was gruesome. Decomposition was severe because the bodies had been submerged in water for quite a few days. Bones appeared, some imbedded in mud, and some still preserved in a soup-like state. I pulled out my jar of Vick's Vapor-Rub and placed a large smear under my nose just as I used to do before an autopsy or opening body bags. Death has a distinct smell, and the stench of decomposition is worse.

After three hours, we were covered in mud and had run out of flags. When I turned around for the first time to look back at the area we had covered, there were thousands of flags sticking out from the mud and debris. I turned to the woman who was working beside me and together we wept. It was all we could do. Close behind us, men were pulling what they could of the debris out of the area so that the bodies could be identified. For the most part, almost all of the flesh and skin was gone.

I wondered what all of these people had been doing before the wall of water had taken them to their deaths. I imagined children playing on the street, mothers working bread, and vendors selling goods. And now those people, the lives of hundreds of thousands of men, women, and children, were marked only by flags notating where the remains of their bodies might be submerged. The image of those thousands of flags sticking out from the muck was branded in my memory that day.

Each subsequent day was filled with different tasks as thousands of aid workers from around the world collectively worked together to bring aid and manage resources being sent to the area.

I was headed to the other side of the country into the territory under the control of the Tamil Tigers, the guerilla faction fighting against government forces. I was quickly briefed on the history of the civil war in Sri Lanka that had created so much unrest and political tension for years in the region. Our job, however, was to identify camp rations, water contamination, and do a needs assessment.

We drove nearly 600 miles to arrive in the territory. Along the way, we were briefed about roadside landmines that had been displaced during the Tsunami and scattered to unknown places. I asked how many had been dislodged by the wave of water, and the answer was astounding. Probably in the tens of thousands according to the military personnel escorting us. It could be more or less, but they didn't know yet. As a precautionary measure, all the camp areas had been checked prior to set up, so we were relatively safe, all things considered.

We visited over 40 camps. The balmy, hot air increased the risk of potential disease, since bacteria and germs thrive in warm, wet climates. Many of the facilities lacked basic toilet areas and sanitation processes, and they were reported and addressed accordingly. We had little access to tents and no dry bedding, our workdays were no less then 17 hours long, and 21 hour days were the norm.

We drove down narrow roads near the now calm waters and witnessed large fishing vessels that had been lifted by the wall of water now laid scattered, helter-skelter, in the middle the roads. There were hundreds of them sprawled before us, a fish monger's graveyard. Some were so far inland it was hard to imagine how they could have ever been in the water at all.

After such a visually horrifying day, it was a relief to head back to the hotel to do some technical work on cataloging survivors, deceased, and familial relations. At the hotel, we debriefed a group of computer company's personnel who were feverishly implementing a database to record survivors and help find family members.

The ugly side of humanity is too often revealed when tragedy strikes. A woman spoke of young children and women who were being kidnapped by underground sex trade and human slave groups, taking advantage of the anonymity of human lives.

This motivated everyone to get these people documented before it was too late. It's difficult to fathom losing my entire family and home to a disaster and finding what one can only assume to be a safe camp, only to be kidnapped, sold, and put on a boat or caravan to be sexually abused for years to come. It's unimaginable to me how some people in this world can be so cruel.

I returned to Tucson permanently affected by the magnitude of despair I had witnessed. The transition back to business as usual was abrupt, making my journey to Sri Lanka seem surreal. I was grateful to be home, no longer smelling death and decay with every breath. For three solid months, World Care and collaborating groups managed to move millions of pounds of aid to the disaster regions. I began focusing on other projects partly to cope with my experience in Sri Lanka.

Not long after I was back in my office, I received a call from Guy Farrow of the Tucson Unified School District. He called to request World Care's formal proposal for the vacant school. It would be presented to the school district's committee for review. I was excited to know that we were actually being considered. We had grown so quickly that our current facility, the former "Silo" building was busting at the seams. The owner of the facility we were occupying had been patient with us for six years, but he now wanted to develop his land, so World Care was over due for relocation. I desperately needed a larger, more permanent place for us, so a move somewhere was inevitable. Mr. Farrow told me that the school district would have an answer for us no later than June. Although I was thrilled that we were being considered, I continued to look for other options, since there were surely other candidates bidding for the same space, and there was no guarantee that it would be ours. In fact, the school was the sixteenth building we had aggressively tried to obtain over the past several years, and each time something had fallen through. But for some reason, I felt hopeful about this school, though I held my breath for good luck (it couldn't hurt).

After the board and I collaborated on a solid proposal, I spent the next few months making appearances at corporations, clubs, and schools, urging their continued support for tsunami victims and thanking them for help they had already provided. The only trip I took abroad that spring was to Chile to supervise the restocking of the clinic I had set up several years earlier.

By early summer, when my workload settled down, I took a trip to visit my family in Chicago. As my flight approached Chicago O'Hare, a severe headache came over me, followed by dizziness. Although the headache shortly subsided, the dizziness continued. I felt sick throughout most of my visit, as though I had a severe sinus infection. When I returned to Tucson, the dizziness came and went, but it wasn't too severe and there was work to be done, so I didn't pay much attention to it.

Our latest local program for Tools for Schools was underway. We had plans to provide a record 24,000 school packs to local kids by August of 2005. The school packs consist of paper, pens, pencils, an eraser, a ruler, recycled binders, a pencil sharpener, glue and a folder. At the same time, it appeared the school board was set to approve our proposal for World Care to receive the building by September, but when they convened in August, the board wanted more. This decision had been up in the air since June. A representative from TUSD phoned on August 8, requesting a presentation be made in front of the school board because there were still some concerns in turning over the building. There were politics involved, including a group of people fighting to keep the building vacant, holding out for "better" use.

Frustrated by the delay, I began working on their request,

in preparation for a top notch presentation to the board. But I was being pulled in several directions and under serious pressure. I was gearing up for an upcoming trip to Indonesia, but had to set my priorities straight. I knew that obtaining that school would allow our organization to run much more smoothly and accomplish so much more, so the proposal was at the top of my list.

CHAPTER TWENTY-FIVE

The Ultimate Test

August 9, 2005

I was sitting at my desk, writing a proposal that would grant World Care the larger space in which to operate, when blood came gushing out of my nose and splattered all over my computer screen. It was something out of _Night of the Living Dead_, only it was clearly real. I got up from my chair and headed for the bathroom, a trail of blood marking my path. I yelled out for anyone who was around, but with the exception of my grant writer, no one else was in the office that day. Thankfully, she came rushing into the bathroom and found me hovered over the sink. I asked her to get some towels as I held my nose. She quickly retrieved what she could find to stop the bleeding. For twenty minutes I bled, and as the blood finally began to subside, a major headache took its place. Fighting an impulse to continue with my project, I decided to call it a day. When I arrived at my home, I felt uncomfortable in my skin. Something was definitely wrong. I soaked rags in hot water and placed them on my forehead to try to relieve the nausea and dizziness that had set in.

My phone rang. It was one of the project managers for

Indonesia wanting to know when I planned to arrive to follow up on the Tsunami project. I told him September, and that I would be coming with another person. I hung up the phone and reflexively picked it up again to dial my doctor. It had to be a sinus infection, it couldn't possibly be anything else, I thought. After describing my symptoms to the nurse on the line, she asked me to come in the next day to be seen. What a nuisance, I thought, but I set up an appointment just the same.

The following morning, I drove to the state-of-the-art clinic at the Veteran's Medical Facility in South Tucson. The nurse went through my medical history and ordered blood work and a CT scan. Having worked in diagnostics for many years, I was pleased with her thoroughness. I waited for the outcome in the lobby.

"Lisa?"

I stood.

"Can you go to room 12? Your nurse, Elaine Hooper, is waiting for you."

Expecting to get my antibiotics and be on my way, I denied the obvious - that the tip of my iceberg had just been exposed. Elaine told me that the blood work and CT scan were negative and that I didn't have a sinus infection. I was shocked -my symptoms were classic - if not a sinus infection, then what? She hurriedly ordered an MR angiogram to be performed the following week. I obliged, and refused to be shaken, it was back to work for me until then.

Throughout the next week, headaches and dizziness came and went, but I didn't let these minor pains get in the way of writing my proposal. The temperature in Tucson was over one hundred degrees, if that wasn't cause for a headache, I didn't know what was. I was rewriting the proposal to the school board for World Care and it needed to be completed for the new space. I simply couldn't afford to be sick. I felt very tired, but attributed it to the heat and stress. In the next week, I needed to move World Care out of our existing location hopefully to the vacant school building. The grant was dependent on this proposal.

The international humanitarian relief organization World Care, that was once six collection boxes in my garage, had accumulated over a million pounds of ongoing resources and supplies that were shipped out on a weekly basis. I started to work out my contingency plans for World Care in case we didn't get the school. Although I'd had a dream that told me we would get the school, I had another that told me that there would be an illness in my family that would bring someone close to death. My dreams since childhood had proven to be premonitions, so I couldn't help but take these recent dreams at more than face value.

I'd begun recording my dreams in 1979, when I dreamt I was standing in purple reeds on water, only to discover my parent's new home in Indiana was covered with the purple reeds from my dream. At the time I had no idea of the meaning of my dream, but had a hunch that I needed to write these dreams down.

But nobody in my family was sick, so my confidence in the predictive nature of my dreams began to wane. I knew that even when I dreamed about successes, I couldn't be complacent. I still had to work hard to achieve my goals.

World Care had overcome tremendous obstacles in a very short period of time, but its future hinged on some key decisions that were in my hands. My board of directors, while supportive and essential for making projects work, had no ability to acquire a building or raise millions to build one. Plus, this simply was not the World Care way. We recycled and used only donated equipment in our operations. By keeping our administrative costs low, we were able to put most of our money directly into projects that helped people. I knew in my heart that we would get the school, but I didn't know when or at what cost. I was also confident that World Care would still exist even if we didn't get the school building, although it would be fragmented around Tucson and prove cumbersome to run. I had to get that school.

I spent six hours in my home office that evening, working out strategies and scenarios until I felt confident that I could negotiate with community business leaders to assist World Care if things fell through. I wasn't giving up the school without a fight. As I prepared for bed, I remembered that my MR angiogram was the next day. I grabbed a towel out of the linen closet on my way to bed, as I had begun to do every night. I warmed it with hot water, placed it on my head, and fell asleep.

Thursday August 18, 2005

I woke up the next morning feeling confident that the proposal would be completed by noon and that I would be able to make my presentation to the board before the end of the month. I went to work, and then around 2:00 p.m. I headed to the hospital for my MRA. Erin, a technologist, was waiting for me. She had been one of my technologists in training when I ran the radiology department at the University of Arizona. I was glad to see her doing so well. A MRA (Magnetic Resonance Angiogram) studies the vessels in the brain and around the body to diagnose different vascular diseases and abnormalities. This was a routine study to follow up on my headaches; at least that's what I told myself. I lay down on the table and Erin advanced me into the large white tube.

Twenty minutes later, I was already on my way home. Like I said, this was no big deal. I was relieved to have the test done and over with, and confident that the results would be normal since the CT scan hadn't shown anything. I stopped at a grocery store on my way home. It hadn't been a half hour since I'd left the hospital when my cell phone rang. I was standing in the cereal aisle, staring at a box of Special K.

"Hello Lisa, this is Dr. Mikail. I don't want to alarm you or get you upset, but your MRA was not normal. You have an aneurysm in your anterior cerebral artery and I need to see you right away."

It took me a second to absorb what he was saying. Then it hit me, and I couldn't believe it. I told him I didn't feel that bad, and asked him what he wanted me to do.

"I want to see you first thing Friday morning in the clinic for blood work, chest X-ray and EKG plus a meeting with the surgeons. I'm scheduling you to meet with a neurosurgeon and a neuro-radiologist."

"I'll be there," I replied, stunned. I hung up the phone and made a beeline for the Cocoa Puffs before heading to the check-out line.

I didn't want to be alone. Still in disbelief, I went to the house of a friend who lived nearby, and told her that I needed to talk. Most of my life I'd been able to deal with things on my own, but this time it was different. I couldn't do this alone. My natural instinct was not to alarm anyone or to panic. I had helped thousands of people go through difficult times during my career in medicine and my work for World Care. And yet, at that moment, I felt completely helpless and vulnerable. Until I spoke to the doctor on Friday, I couldn't be sure about anything, and this gave me solace. I wanted to believe that they must have misread the films. I told myself I was fine.

I felt fine, except for a slight headache. But on Friday,

after meeting with the doctors, I learned that I had a time bomb in my head.

"Lisa, this is very serious. You must have surgery right away. You have few options. Due to the location of the aneurysm we need a closer look, but you may lose your right eye. We need to map the vessel before we do the surgery to determine how to proceed."

I told the surgeon I wanted a second opinion, which he said wasn't a problem, but I had to have it done within the next forty-eight hours because of the urgency. I couldn't delay it anymore. The surgeon explained that the vessel was far into the brain and a craniotomy would be too risky; the chance of a stroke was very high. At that point, I stepped outside of myself as if I was watching a movie of my own life. The distance allowed me to be moderately reasonable.

I asked to see the films. I wanted to know how my doctors assessed the risk of performing surgery on me. I had spent seventeen years of my radiology career looking at blood vessels and performing the very diagnostic procedures these doctors were viewing so I understood the risks. I knew it had to do with numbers, age, mortality rate and general health, but what I really wanted to know was whether or not the surgery could possibly leave me with brain damage.

The doctor sat me down and told me to make sure my personal affairs were in order before the surgery. My chances of survival with this surgery were slim, and if I did survive, the possibility of brain damage would be high.

I told him no way. I was not having a craniotomy and I insisted on looking into other procedures. The newest procedure was microsurgery platinum or titanium coil deployment into the aneurysm. That too, I was told, was risky, but it was much less invasive. I agreed to go with that surgery if the second opinion agreed that it was the best option. My friend at the university agreed to review my films on Monday. The surgery would have to be postponed for those precious forty-eight hours.

I hardly slept that night and awoke early the next day to get my things in order. I had to handle my personal affairs, including my will, plus meet with the second opinion doctors and then there was work! I had to meet with the school district people to go over the building needs. My presentation to the school board had been set for August 24, and there was no way I was backing out.

Sunday August 21, 2005

I called my mom as I always do, for our weekly chat. I didn't want to alarm her, but with much persistence from friends, I told her that I had been diagnosed with a brain aneurysm and asked if she could come take care of me that week. Without hesitation, she made arrangements to fly to Tucson on Tuesday morning. I spent the rest of the day trying to relax, going over my personal papers and putting together notes for an emergency World Care meeting on Tuesday.

As I wrote up the agenda, looking out at the beautiful mountains that filled my back windows, I said a prayer. I thanked God for all of the wonderful things and people that had been given to me to learn from in my life, and the dreams that had inspired me to help others. I asked myself if I had any regrets in life, and my answer was no. I realized that all the things I had gone through were life lessons, and if it was my time to go, I would have no regrets other than my wish to see World Care grow to the full potential that I had imagined in my reoccurring dreams. My faith in God and the universe was strong and I knew that I would know soon enough what my fate would be. There was nothing else I could do but make sure my family, World Care, and personal obligations were taken care of. I finished my tasks, and then began to cry.

On Monday, I received a call from my surgeon. He wanted me to be in the hospital on Wednesday morning for the angiogram and prep for the surgery the following day. Then I went for the second opinion. Although both sides agreed that I had an aneurysm, there were disagreements as to the technique, and the effect on my right eye. It was thought by one radiologist that I could lose the sight in my right eye because the artery that feeds it was involved and would possibly be severed when they tried to repair the aneurysm. I asked to see my films.

Dr. Siegal leaned over the table and pointed at the images of my head. "Lisa, the location of the aneurysm is millimeters from your right optic artery which provides blood to your right eye. We believe you could lose the right eye entirely."

As I looked closer something inside me did not agree.

"Doc, I have to tell you, I am not losing my eye. I am not interested in hearing what I am going to lose. I want to see my options. What are my damn options?

I sat back in the chair, realizing my composure was slipping and I needed to take a step back. Dr. Siegal turned with a somber look on his face, "No mistake Lisa, this is very serious. Losing your eye is the least of the potential complications. You know this. I am sorry.

Deep down I knew he was right. As a professional I knew what could happen. I just wasn't ready to leave earth yet. I did not want that to be an option. But it was.

After discussion, the doctors and I agreed on a procedure that we all felt comfortable with under the circumstances. Surgery would be scheduled as soon as possible.

I went to work on Tuesday as usual, and picked up Mom at the airport around noon. Then we headed over to the hospital for some more tests before the surgery. I received a call from my surgeon informing me the surgery was scheduled for Wednesday. I told the doctor that I needed one more day to work some things out and I would be in their hands on Thursday. They didn't want to push the surgery off any further, plus there was difficulty with scheduling, but I insisted that I needed one more day to handle my affairs. If I were to die in the operating room, at least I'd have one more day. They told me that they would let me know Wednesday morning. If the surgery couldn't be rescheduled, I had to be there by noon.

I spoke with the World Care board of directors on Tuesday, letting them know what was happening, and turning the organization's operations and direction over to the officers indefinitely. For several years we had been setting up the infrastructure to handle this very type of emergency, and now we were putting it to the test. I hoped that the mission of the organization could be carried on in my absence. I asked the Board to keep my condition confidential. I did not want the school board to make any negative decisions about us acquiring the school because of my uncertain status.

I also didn't want my own Board to know exactly how serious this was because I was concerned that a couple of members didn't have World Care's best interest in mind. The thought of them carrying out World Care's mission without me - if I didn't make it - well, I couldn't fathom it. If we didn't get the school, and I died in the operating room, or worse yet became brain damaged, all else would be moot, anyway.

We adjourned the meeting around 6:30 p.m. Mom and I were silent in the car on the ride home. At home we got into our pajamas and lounged in the living room. It was then my mind began to think about the seriousness of what was about to happen and how little, if any, control I had in its outcome. I was thankful to have her there to help me through the huge amount of uncertainty and stress I was facing. When I expressed my concerns to my mother, she responded, "Honey, you've built a great thing. I am so proud of you. When you create something successful, you'll spend the rest of your life protecting it. You must be aware of people's motives. Even though you are a humanitarian, you can't trust everyone. But let's not worry about that right now. You have enough to deal with already."

Mom's words comforted me, and just then, my sister Cathy rang. "Hey, just want to let you know Peter and I are on our way out on the next flight. How are you feeling?" Peter is Mom's husband.

"I'm pretty good, all things considered," I replied.

I felt relieved that she and Peter were coming soon. I was concerned for my mother because she doesn't do well with doctors. If something happened to me, I knew Cathy would handle our family matters. That's been our pact with each other. Mom gently caressed my arm, letting me know that she was there for me.

"I love you Mom."

"I love you too, honey."

August 24, 2005

On Wednesday, I headed to the hospital to take care of the remaining second opinion issues with the surgeon, and also to see what else I needed to do. At 3:00 p.m. the doctors confirmed that my surgery had been moved to Thursday. I thanked the surgeon, and told him to get a good night's sleep so he could be well rested and alert when he worked on my head. It didn't help that he had only performed five of these procedures prior to mine.

He assured me that he felt good about it, so I relaxed, a little. I felt somewhat relieved to have everything on the medical side of things in order, and I knew that World Care was taken care of, too. Now all I had to do was get that school building!

Mom and I headed over to the meeting with the school board around 4:30 that afternoon, but not before popping into Dillard's to freshen up at the makeup counter, since I hadn't had enough time to go home and get ready prior to the meeting. Mom went shopping while I was being "made over," and managed to find a few things I might need for the hospital. As for me, a dip in the fountain of youth couldn't have helped me then, but the makeover at least managed to perk up my complexion a little bit. When we arrived, people were already assembling in the board room and community members were coming in to listen to my presentation, and to vote. Board members and VIP's were seated in the front row. News crews were outside waiting to hear the verdict. I resigned myself to the understanding that what was meant to be, would be. If World Care was not meant to get the school, then there was nothing I could do about it. I put my faith in the universe and hoped for the best.

I took a deep breath and prayed for guidance as I walked calmly to the podium in the center of the room. There were a lot of people there to support us. I felt it was my responsibility to not let them down. For the first time my Mother was here to see what World Care was all about and what it meant to me and the community. The room became silent as I approached the microphone.

"Good evening everyone. I am Lisa Hopper, CEO/Founder of World Care, a humanitarian aid organization that supports TUSD and the community of Tucson... I am not here to convince you or plea for your pity of why World Care should get the school, I am asking for your support because it's the right thing to do for the school district and for the community and people around the world."

As I made my presentation along with the community supporters, each school board member, with the exception of one, submitted a positive ballot for World Care. Once the final vote was approved, everyone in the room applauded. My eyes filled with tears as I was bombarded with congratulations. After a few minutes with the media, a small group of us headed to a bar on University Boulevard to celebrate. World Care was going to have a permanent home after all. I felt confident that I had accomplished everything I had set out to do before my surgery.

As we celebrated our victory of getting the school, my thoughts wandered. What will tomorrow bring? Will I see my 44th Birthday?

The morning came quickly. Mom and I headed to the VA Hospital. The nursing staff greeted us with smiles as they began to prepare me for the procedure. I kissed my mom and reassured her everything was going to be fine and not to worry. Several doctors entered the room as the anesthesiologist pushed medication in my I.V.

"Lisa you're going to feel sleepy. We'll see you when you wake up."

I was trying to count backwards, and then a long white tunnel appeared.

CHAPTER TWENTY-SIX

The Wait

Thursday August 25, 2005

Faint beeping sounds muttered in the distance as I began to come too. My eyes were heavy and blurred as I tried to force them open. My mind could not connect with familiar objects as I was unaware of my surroundings. As though no time had passed at all, things began to click. One voice then two voices shuttered my brain. Then I began to drift in and out of consciousness. If something had happened to me, I was too weak to care.

"She might need a few more hours rest," the unfamiliar voice warned. I heard a door close but felt the presence of others around me still.

"She's still unconscious. Oh God, I can't do this." I recognized my sister Cathy's voice as if it were my own. Then I felt the weight of someone next to me. I became aware of the bed I was lying in. A hospital bed, I guessed.

"Well, do you think she'll be okay?" My mother sounded concerned.

"When she wakes up we'll know," Cathy answered. "Where did the doctor go? I want to talk to the doctor."

I tried to open my eyes, or move my arm, or utter a single solitary word, and all of those things felt impossible. Sleep was all I could do, so I gave in to it. My family eventually left the room. I fell into a deep, dark sleep for the next seven hours.

Then my eyes opened abruptly, as if I'd been having a nightmare. My head was packed in ice. I felt like I had been dreaming for days. I could tell that I was no longer dreaming. The hospital room was real. I looked around the room decorated in mauve and tan. I was hesitant to move my head, although my mind raced. I was thinking clearly and rationally, a good sign. But what had happened? I fought hard to remember. I looked around for the call button to get a nurse's attention. Maybe a nurse could help put the pieces together.

A male nurse entered and spoke in a quiet voice, "Well, you've been out for a while. Are you in any pain?"

I took a quick inventory of my body and felt no pain. I wondered what kind of drugs I was probably on, and how I would feel when they wore off. "No pain," I responded. Then my stomach growled. I was starving!

"Can I eat?" I asked, "Is my family here?"

"Yes," he replied, "You can eat, but no, your family went home to rest. It's two o'clock in the morning. You gave them quite a scare. They'll be here in a few hours. For now, just rest, take it easy."

"How long have I been sleeping?" It felt like days. And the way I said it must have alerted him.

The nurse hesitated for a minute and then began, "Lisa, you suffered from a brain aneurysm. The top doctors in this hospital performed a state-of-the-art surgery more than twenty-four hours ago. The surgery lasted three hours."

"Brain aneurysm?" I repeated. The facts came rushing back to me. The procedure, the doctors, everything. Titanium coils were placed into the aneurysm to cut off the pressure and streamline the blood flow to the right hemisphere of my brain.

Right then, an excruciating pain attacked my head, I'd never felt anything like it in my life. I became nauseous and dizzy and felt myself slipping away. I tried to focus on the male nurse who was still in the room, but his image and everything else became blurry around me. I fought hard to remain conscious. To fight through the pain and dizziness that had come over me. Then I was out again.

Time passed. It could have been five minutes or five hours, I was still somewhat unconscious when I began thrashing about in the bed. Then doctors entered the room and wheeled me off down a hall. I later found out that they performed an emergency CT scan to see if the aneurysm had ruptured in my brain. The scan was negative and so the surgery held, just took some time to get used to it, I guess.

They found the right drugs to stop the pain and the nausea. I stopped thrashing and vomiting and fell back asleep. Hours passed and I was starting to return to normal. By the next morning, I felt like a new woman. I had minimal pressure in my head and again felt hungry. The nurses were wonderful and accommodating. They filled me with fluids and were very attentive. What more could a girl with a box of ice around her head ask for?

I was hooked up to all kinds of IVs and monitors. As I

watched the nurse walking away, I remembered what the male nurse had explained to me sometime earlier. The aneurysm. In my mind, I began naming every object in the room to detect if my brain was functioning properly. There was a table, two chairs, a lamp, and a television. I was golden. My head felt like it weighed a hundred pounds. I couldn't lift it, yet I felt overjoyed that I had survived the aneurysm and the surgery. I silently thanked God for keeping me around a little longer, and then drifted off to sleep.

The following morning, the doctor informed me that I would make a full recovery, and that he could release me from the hospital provided I would rest for the next month. I agreed to rest, and began to prepare for my departure. I knew the drill from my experience working in hospitals. As soon as I could pee and get off all of the monitors, I could go home. Make room for someone else who needed help.

Mom came into the room then and gave me a huge hug and kisses. I was so happy to see her. The rest of my family followed and helped me gather my things to take home. I was still drugged and unsteady, but eager and ready to leave. I bid everyone at the hospital a grateful farewell. My mother wheeled me out to the car in the hospital wheelchair.

I was released a day short of my 44th birthday shared with my twin sister Cathy. We decided to celebrate early. It just felt right. For the first time in my life, simply being alive was the greatest gift I'd ever received. I was grateful to share another birthday with family and friends. My family stayed with me, making sure I was going to be fine before they left for Chicago.

I spent the next two weeks recovering in and around my bed. No televisions, no newspapers, just nature. I left everything stressful behind me in an attempt to totally unwind, strictly following the doctor's orders. A deliberately slow walk through the desert was all the exercise I allowed myself for a while.

The day after my real birthday, Pam called from World Care.

"Happy Birthday, Lisa!" she exclaimed, although she quickly explained the reason for her call. "We didn't want to bother you, because the doctor doesn't want you getting upset, but this is important. A huge hurricane called Katrina just hit the Delta coast, mainly Louisiana and Mississippi. What's the call?" Yah, this is what we do. Have we had calls from the community to respond? Yes. Get the board to help out."

Despite the urgency of the situation, I didn't feel panicked. I knew that World Care could be fully operational even in my absence. We had spent a lot of time and energy building our emergency programs so that they could be put into action at the bat of an eye. Although it was the beginning of the school year and World Care was busy with "Tools for Schools," collecting and distributing school supplies to over 25,000 local students, we responded immediately and without a moment's hesitation to the Katrina disaster.

NBC News reported that World Care provided the single largest civilian response in the United States! This marked a shift in World Care's evolution. It was clear to me that the organization would continue to provide humanitarian support to people in need, but the larger picture would require us to share our methods and influence other existing organizations to adopt our effective processes so that the worldwide humanitarian aid network could grow.

The impact that World Care had on the Katrina relief effort was due in part to the fact that we are an NGO, granting us the ability to cut through the red tape and get to the heart of the disaster with a clear strategy for relief, supply shipments, and humanitarian aid.

With an urgent sense of my own mortality, and also an understanding of the impact we were having on people in need, it became clear that my focus needed to shift. I no longer had to figure out how to run World Care; instead I had to figure out how to teach others to run it in my absence, so that it could continue its legacy beyond my personal limitations. On national television, NBC validated that our models worked effectively. It was the impetus I needed to realize World Care's new direction. It was time to teach our methods to other organizations with like-minded humanitarian goals.

My brush with death made me realize that World Care is one link of many in a web of relief organizations worldwide, and it is our responsibility to share what works for us with others, for humanity's sake.

The aneurysm humbled me by showing me how little in life I can control. It also opened my heart and made me thankful beyond words that I had listened to my dreams and intuition. In one year, I had experienced the most devastating disasters that our world had ever known--the tsunami, Katrina, and the Pakistan earthquake, which followed in October. Within a twenty-four hour period on August 25, I had seen my life flash before my eyes, along with all of my hopes and dreams for World Care. I felt grateful and truly blessed that I was alive at all; truly fortunate to be living and breathing my vision of social change and humanitarian aid every single day.

My optimism was vigorously renewed, and my faith that everything in my life was as it should be grew more vital than ever before. With a new location on the horizon for World Care, a magical sense of purpose emerged from the tumultuous year. The question lingered in my mine, "would I be able to work at the level I did before?"

It was unclear what my long term prognosis was from the

doctor or if I would ever be able to travel by air again. I needed answers and I needed them soon.

PART THREE

CHAPTER TWENTY-SEVEN

Awake and Still Dreaming

It was June 2006, the beginning of the hot season in Arizona. As I stood on my back patio at 2:00 a.m. the moon was full. My sleeping patterns had been off since surgery. It was so bright that for a moment, I mistakenly thought that the porch light had been left on. The Catalina Mountains were silhouetted against the moonlit sky, the smell of creosote lingered in the air, the aftermath of a summer monsoon's outpouring on the desert floor. The soothing silence of the night put me at ease.

Life after a brain aneurysm leaves a person to wonder who really is in charge. After all, I was given a second chance at life. I thought about the dream I'd had in which a person very close to me would become very ill. I realized it was me. To me this was another confirmation of the power of dreams. Still, it was hard to believe that I'd had an aneurysm of any kind, let alone one in my brain. I guess I'm one of the fortunate ones so far. No debilitation with the exception of a little tenderness and numbing on the right side of my head. Since the operation, I've been enjoying life immensely, with fewer headaches as time passes. 2006 proved to be a year of clarity and change. Thirteen years had passed since

I had the first World Care dream. It was taking me longer that I expected to recover. My brain was readjusting the flow of blood. My stamina was at half mast. It was as if my eight cylinder engine was knocked down to only four. I was running a little slower than usual, but I was grateful for life.

Having survived the surgery, I wanted to know what the prognosis was concerning the coils and what complications may arise. My doctor kept close watch on me during my recovery. He gave me what little information he had:

"The coils are a very new product being used. Very little is known of the long-term outcome at this point in time."

Does that make me the guinea pig? "Well, I can't be concerned with what we don't yet know, I guess. Can you tell me if I will have any limitations in terms of movement or brain function?" "Lisa, as long as you take good care of yourself, you'll be fine. No extreme sports or stress on your body. Don't go jumping out of airplanes or scuba diving now. You understand, of course."

I uttered a half laugh, but his words didn't strike me as funny at all. I reminded him of the type of work I do, often requiring long trips overseas to dangerous areas.

"Your lifestyle is going to have to be altered a little. You'll have to slow it down," he responded.

"How?" I wanted to know, "In what ways can I alter my career exactly?" I had already made a mental list of the activities I planned to resume–things I had enjoyed doing prior to the onset of the headaches. There was golf, running, hiking, and kickboxing, to name a few.

"Well you are going to have to pay more attention to your activities," he cautioned. "Long flights overseas could be your

undoing. Kickboxing is not a good idea, neither is scuba diving."
His list went on, longer than mine. He concluded with the
poignant "I recommend you learn to relax and enjoy life more."

Gee, thanks.

I didn't bother explaining to him the many ways I already
enjoyed my life, instead I had to look at my life in a different way.
My life had been forever changed by the aneurysm. I hadn't seen
the error in my previous ways--namely, how frenzied a life I was
leading--the pace of my life had been sucking me dry. It wasn't
until I was forced to push the stop button and do close to nothing
that it all became clear. In order to recuperate from the harsh
pace I'd set for myself, I started painting, reading for pleasure, and
setting small short term goals to regain my strength and physical
coordination.

I hadn't realized how sick I'd been until I started feeling
better. I felt lost without a million things to juggle, but slowly,
the habitual desire for stress, speed, and pressure began to change
into a desire for calmness and tranquility. Letting go is not easy,
but very necessary to make life more enjoyable. I'd spent most
of my life focusing on other people's needs; now I needed to
bring balance back into my own life. World Care was getting
acquainted with its new home, and there was still much to be
done.

My new goal was to allow the systems in place to proceed
naturally, then to formalize the organization from a managerial
perspective. Since I had managed large hospital departments,
I knew what had to be done. We were still operating with a
skeletal staff and some departments had to be reorganized so that
no one person had autonomous control over the systems. At
that point however, World Care's volunteers were already over
five hundred strong, so I was confident that we could overcome
whatever obstacles we might face. I made a list of everything that

needed to be done and began ticking off the goals. A new board president was elected and he too had already begun drafting a list for changes to be made.

While some people within the organization were reluctant to modify, adapt, and evolve, World Care was moving to the next level whether they liked it or not. My years of training in the military and practice in hospitals and around the world had taught me to play hardball. Imagine that.

Despite my tough outer shell, I started missing my family in Chicago. It had been nearing a year since my operation when I'd last seen them. That spring, I took a trip home and made a point to go back more often to connect with my sisters and friends from then on. Seeing everyone back home was like a battery recharge for the soul. It was my favorite kind of vacation. It's never too late to bond with family and old friends, I realized. It had been nearly twenty-seven years since I'd left Chicago for the military, but whenever I made it back there, I felt at home. It was almost like I'd never left.

The University of Arizona offered me a part time teaching position working with Honors students across a variety of majors. I had been providing internship opportunities to students through World Care for several years by then, and felt honored to be given the chance to teach in a formal, classroom setting. Since I was still unable to return to my normal level of activity, I accepted the offer to teach just one day per week. The hours could increase gradually in congruence with my recovery. With free reign on classroom topics, I chose to focus on social entrepreneurs in international arenas and to educate students on countries, customs, and cultures as they relate to international aid. I scribbled notes, brainstorming the ways in which certain aspects of the world work within my World Care realm. The class became structured in a sense, using World Care as the model and example for this interdisciplinary study on society.

As quickly as the fall semester began, the students became eager to sign up for real programs outside of their academic, more theoretical-based learning. In one assignment, the class was broken up into teams and each team was assigned to facilitate an international project. One such project was the Democratic People's Republic of Congo's aids clinic and birthing center. The students excelled far beyond my expectations in not only managing the project but also designing the facility. I was floored; these students were onto something. After submitting the assignment to the company heading up the real-life project in the DPR Congo, the company took on the project as the primary design for the structure.

All I want for Christmas is no more headaches!

As we headed swiftly into 2007, 2006 was closing on a high note, or so I thought. I had made arrangements to head back to Chicago for the Christmas holiday. Two days before I was scheduled to leave, I suffered severe swelling on the right side of my head. My first thought was that I'd been bitten by an insect while I was working in the yard, but when the swelling didn't improve after a day on ice, I called my doctor. He asked me to come to his office.

"You've suffered a stroke, Lisa."

I was shocked. Considering my recent medical history, I probably shouldn't have been as utterly surprised as I was. The doctor explained that the stroke had affected my right eye and facial muscles. I was scared and frustrated but also relieved that it hadn't been worse. The doctor informed me then that this wasn't uncommon after the type of surgery I'd recently undergone.

The stroke didn't kill me either, and only caused a few days' delay on my trip to Chicago. I waited for some of the symptoms to subside, then left for a couple of weeks to be with family and friends. I felt fine but my face still needed time to recover. It looked a little distorted but didn't bother me beyond the physical appearance. It certainly wasn't enough for me to postpone my trip any further. In fact, that trip home was one of the best times I'd ever had, surrounded by the people I love, having overcome not only a brain aneurysm but also a stroke. I felt a heightened sense of presence and engagement with everyone like never before. That New Year's Eve, my friends and family surprised me with football tickets to the Bears game. At the end of the game, we watched fireworks explode in the night's sky, from the top of Soldier Field overlooking the Chicago skyline, the snow falling softly in a dreamy sort of way. Sharing that moment with the people I love was precious, a memory I'll keep with me always.

CHAPTER TWENTY-EIGHT

Returning to World Care's Mission

I was scheduled to embark on my journey to the Congo in five hours. World Care had already begun to build a hospital for aids patients and their babies, but the project had been postponed due to fighting in the region. Since the fighting had ceased, the project was allowed to resume. I was traveling to the Congo to conduct the assessment in order to set the wheels in motion once more. This would be my first international trip since my surgery. Of course, I felt a little uneasy about how my body would react to the pressure of the airplane over such a long span of time.

As I prepared for the trip, I reflected back on the past thirteen years since World Care began in my garage. The progress we'd made astounded me, it stretched far beyond my expectations of the organization. In my wildest dreams (and there have been some wild ones), I couldn't have imagined the rate of growth and success we'd already achieved. I had traveled to over 26 countries, and had conducted research on over 70 nations! For thirteen years, I had seen people all over the world suffer in pain; dying from starvation, disease, poverty, and murder. I'd seen poverty fueled by greed for land and oil, politics, and differences in nationality, race, and religion. Yet scattered among the myriad of humanitarian disgraces were seeds of hope. I'd seen the best and worst that humanity had to offer. Despite even the most despicable acts of humans and governing societies, who act out of hatred and fear, there also exists incredible love and compassion on the opposite end of the scale. A strong sense of compassion is a driving force that exists among those of us who cannot remain complacent, and seek to counteract corrupt practices and mistreatment of various groups of people around the world.

To do nothing would mean that we have given up on salvation. Someone once told me that when Pandora opened up the infamous box, many awful things were unleashed into this world, but also unleashed was hope.

Today, I understand much more about the ways in which the humanitarian aid machine works than I had thirteen years ago. Armed with this knowledge, I feel even more determined to continue my work in the face of unforeseen challenges to the non-profit world as it continues to correct past mistakes and to improve on accountability. The learning curve is endless in such an endeavor but all we can do is continue to adapt and provide aid where it is needed. While lack of oversight is the main perpetrator of corruption and still runs rampant in the non-profit world today, we now have the tools in place to curb this effect. I have faith that goodwill will prevail.

I would arrive in the Democratic Republic of Congo (Zaire) with a much more discriminating purpose in mind.

I was walking into a freshly democratic country. Joseph Kabila had successfully won the election, making him the first democratically elected president in Zaire. Kabila's opponent was Bemba, estimated to have had close to 3,000 followers. This is modest compared to the population of over a million in the local vicinity but an alarming number, considering that Bemba's supporters were, for the most part, armed and dangerous. They finally ceased their bomb and terror campaign and retreated back into the jungles of the Congo after the election results were announced. Bemba actually moved to Portugal on medical leave after failing in an attempt to overthrow the newly elected President in March of 2006.

Although the political climate was noticeably calmer than it had been a few months earlier, the Congo was still considered to be the third most volatile nation in the world.

I read through several detailed accounts of the recent history in the region as I snuggled up in my airplane seat for the long flight to Africa.

The hospital I had plans to assess was nestled in the western region of the DRC called Matadi. Its hillsides hug the Nile River as the muddy, brown waters flow determinedly into the jungle. The Midema wheat mill stands tall along the riverbed, producing the majority of the country's supply of fortified flour, distributed across the Congo. About a kilometer away from the mill lays the Port of Matadi, pulling in sea-going containers of produce, ore, and wood products, among other import and export goods. Thousands of containers stacked three stories high fill the docks each day, awaiting rides inland or outbound onto the Atlantic Ocean.

Upon my arrival, Jakob, a young Congolese man who had been hired by the Mill to drive me around, greeted me at the airport. I was thankful he spoke broken English and was well versed on the community activities. The airport looked ancient and unkempt. I couldn't help but wonder if it was a sign of what was to come. Masses of people were everywhere. There was probably order among the chaos, though none that I could readily point out. Quickly, I learned that the order that existed in this country was centered on payoffs.

We were shuffled out of the airport by the movement of the crowd, and approached a Mill car while still awaiting my bag. It was retrieved at the cost of USD $2.00, the equivalent of a two-day wage for a working Congolese person. As I was being pushed through the airport exit by the massive crowd, I came face-to-face with a Frenchman who offered some words of advice.

"Be careful," he warned, "what lies beneath the surface remains to be seen. There is enough hell here to go around. All help is kindly welcomed."

I wasn't sure what to make of the man's admonition.

Fortunately, Jakob was a friend of the custom's officials, so processing my entrance went smoothly. Outside of the old airport, the air was sticky and muggy. There were so many crowds of people moving in various directions, that it reminded me of ants working around a massive colony. I couldn't get the picture out of my head. Maybe it was very American or arrogant of me to think this way, but it made the transition easier. Police were well dressed and very present in the mob scene. There were additional convoys of military personnel decked out in green SWAT gear with machine guns, semi-automatics, and handguns draped from their already intimidating uniforms. The cars pulling up to the curb were either luxury European vehicles, or indistinguishable vans that operated as taxis, crammed full with as many people as possible.

I was thankful for my window seat on the drive through town. The streets were alive at night; vendors sat curbside selling fruit, wooden carvings, homemade jewelry, sugar, used clothing, and household goods. Women balanced their belongings atop their heads with little effort and beautiful grace. We must have passed thousands of people moving vigorously, heading somewhere, while thousands more just lingered around piles of burning garbage. In the glow of the fires, I could make out only the bare outlines of shanty houses that seemed to go on forever. Children were running all around the streets, and I wondered how many of them were homeless.

Driving toward the middle of town, I probed Jakob about what his life was like before he started working for the humanitarian organization. He explained that he'd been a miner before switching over to this field: "The mines I was working in, the Shinkolobwe mines in the south province of Lubumbashi, produce uranium U235 and U238."

My radiology background told me why it was obvious he no longer wanted to work for the mining industry in this country. The type of uranium they were mining is a heavy-weighted isotope that can produce enough energy to supply a nuclear bomb. Jakob told me that when the economy fell through, the mining industry was in shambles. At that time, even the warlords were having trouble dumping their supplies. Later on, in the late 1990's, it had been rumored that North Korea had purchased the U235 and other products of equal strength for a deeply discounted price.

Jakob had already lost several of his family members to the mines, so when he had an opportunity to escape, he fled to Kinshasa. I can only imagine what had happened to his family, working in such harsh conditions. He was happy to have steady work for a change, making $2.50 per day, a far better wage than the majority of the Congolese who were unemployed. His pay was also higher than regular laborers who earned only $1.00 per day.

The following morning, as the first rays of sunlight struck the walls through the hotel window, I felt hopeful that I could contribute to the quality of life for the people of this region. I felt a slight headache and a dribble of blood ran down from my nose as I got up from bed. It was a reminder of what I had been spared two years earlier. Careful that no water entered my mouth from possible unsanitary conditions, I submerged my head under the warm spray in the shower to remedy the bloody nose.

A car was already waiting outside as I entered the lobby of the hotel. to take me to the Midema office. Midema is one of the strongest companies in the Congo, providing flour to the entire country. Despite tension and political unrest in March of 2007, the company persevered and continues to be one of the driving forces of the Congolese economy. Most of their smaller competitors had disappeared entirely during the political uprising, along with many other corporations in different industries.

We hit the ground running as I met Eva, a petite New Yorker, tough as nails, who would be my guide for the next week. She debriefed me on our itinerary, which included a meeting with President Kabila. Most of my work would entail observation, insight, practical systems implementation, and evaluations of the medical systems and conditions. The purpose of my trip was to do a needs-assessment of an existing area that would in turn provide detailed information about what would be necessary to bring the facility up to state-of-the-art medical standards. The Congo would be a challenging project since I not only had to assess the physical structure of the facility, but also the political situation, disease levels, and corruption.

As the days passed, I felt that despite the political unrest, insurmountable government bureaucracy, and faulty information, there was hope in Mitadi. The doctors, nurses, and medical staff worked diligently each day in their efforts to fight malaria in children, and collecting data from aids patients in order to deliver proper treatments. Hundreds of patients passed through the doors of medical clinics each week, and the doctors valiantly worked to make the most of what little supplies they had.

Until very recently, small provinces, such as Kabula, took in very little tax returns, since tax money for the most part remained in the capital. With the change in government, forty percent of the local taxes now remained in circulation in the small provinces. For the first time in decades, public works improvements were being made in areas that had been previously overlooked. Roads were being paved both literally and metaphorically, and community improvement construction was underway across the Congo, which is the size of Texas but only had three hundred miles of paved roads prior to the improvements.

A good look at the health providers in any community can tell you a lot about the community as a whole. The financial status, corruption, diseases, nutrition, air pollutants, death rates and sanitation conditions also indicate specific community needs. My mind has been conditioned to analyze environments in order to figure out ways to help people on a scale that many people would perceive as impossibly large. As I witnessed the alarmingly vast amounts of poverty and illness around me, I reminded myself that nothing is impossible.

There was little to no electricity, with the exception of government-run facilities and a few select powerhouse corporations. Most of the existing electricity came from hydroelectric power produced by the Anga Dam, run by Western Corridor (WESTCOR) and located just north of Matadi, on the west coast of the Nile. Interestingly, just six percent of the energy generated by the dam is being used by the Congo, which begs the question, where is the other ninety-four percent going? A $14 million feasibility study was funded by the African Development Bank to back a proposed six to eight billion dollar upgrade to the facility to generate more wattage to be sold to South Africa.

Selling energy is big business on this continent. Construction on the upgrade was set to begin in 2009, and to be completed by 2015-in the meantime, there are additional projects going on to increase the energy output of other dams to generate energy for the WESTCOR grid system. My hope is that the city of Matadi will eventually have access to more of the energy produced by its resources.

Eva interrupted my contemplation to inform us that our meeting with the President had been canceled because an emergency Senate session had been called. Apparently, President Kabila's former opponent, Bemba, had requested to extend his leave to Portugal past the ninety-day provision, after which he would lose his seat in the senate. Bemba, who had orchestrated the most recent violent uprising, and who owned many companies including media stations and massive real estate within the country, was the type of guy who would put up a fight if he didn't get what he wanted. He could easily create another uprising if he lost his senate seat.

On our way to the USAID offices, in the central part of Kinshasa, we passed a large plot of land covered in blue tarps, surrounded by fencing, with no signs. I was told that this was to be the new Chinese Embassy. For security reasons, only Chinese workers were allowed on site to build. The precautions were necessary, considering that palm oil and diamonds were major exports, and in exchange, it was no secret that China had turned Africa into its dumping grounds for their product rejects.

We arrived at the USAID office and met with one of the directors. I was there to discuss aids and HIV programs that were underway in the country. I assumed that since aids had been around for 30 years, and since billions of dollars had been poured into the country to fight the epidemic, that there would be a fairly aggressive testing and treatment program already in place. I couldn't have been more wrong. The statistics that the director had given me were apparently created out of guesswork, there was nothing concrete. Nothing matched up, and when confronted about this, the director talked in circles until I could no longer listen.

His attention was fixed on a bullet hole that scarred his desk, the result of gunfire during the latest uprising in March. He had been standing at the time of the shooting. Had he been sitting at his desk, he'd have undoubtedly been killed. Luckily he had gotten up to photocopy some documents when the shots were fired and his life was spared. It was clear to me that this man felt defeated in his efforts to surmount the aids crisis, his focus now permanently affixed on his extraordinarily close encounter with his own murder.

I became irritated after spending over an hour asking the man for something other than percentages, to no avail. I wanted base numbers from which the office had been testing, he wanted to stare at the bullet hole. After I informed him that we were writing his office into a grant for funding, he began to open up with more concrete figures. Even so, his numbers didn't add up to the amount of funding his offices had already been issued. It was revealed that the system was deeply flawed and what little data they'd kept proved to be inaccurate.

After hitting our first dead end, we recalculated our route and headed to the Family Health Initiative (FHI), another group providing testing and minimal treatment to aids patients. Minimal treatment meant that there was only one person on the job. Warehouses amounts of pharmaceutical products that had been purchased by the government to treat people with HIV and aids had been destroyed because the distribution bottleneck was so great that much of the medicine was out of date before it could be sent to where it was needed. While massive cash was being sent to pharmaceutical companies to produce drugs needed for treatment, very little funding was allotted to delivery and distribution sectors. The preventative measures of education and testing were also severely under-funded.

We returned to the hospital in Matadi where I met some of the patients. Six children were being treated for malaria in the pediatric ward, and the adults had malaria, dysentery, and HIV. I wondered if it was possible for one person to make a difference in a world in which there were so many suffering, and even more shielding their eyes from poverty.

The history of the Congo shows that it is possible for one person to destroy a country. In the 1970's, President Mobutu single-handedly brought a country down from promise, wealth, and hope, to horror. Mobutu nationalized major industries built by foreign investors, then kicked the investors out of the country and distributed their jobs to his unqualified friends and family who, not surprisingly, ran the economy into the ground. It was economic suicide. Civil war ensued. Corruption and lawlessness took hold of infrastructure and education, causing any semblance of order to collapse. Disease, rape, and murder became ways of life. It is possible for one person to make a difference, but that difference is not always good.

Today, with few large companies present to support mass employment, most communities earn their livelihood through micro-businesses created by product distributors, selling mostly substandard products usually pedaled on the streets. Used products line the dirt walkways, displayed neatly in a row, their version of department stores in high-end European malls. I see hope in the eyes of the proprietors managing their inventory, haggling for every dollar they can get. They have their dreams just as I have mine, and no one should be denied the pursuit of their dreams, no matter how modest.

Several hours before my departure, we debriefed my assessment in order to plan for the next steps of the project. At the airport, I watched as airport police pulled semi-automatic machine guns from two cars that entered the vicinity. I justified my discrete but illegal public photographs on the looseness of the laws. Just in case, I had brought two cameras with me. I hoped that the photos would make it home. My driver walked me through the airport. I had to pay $30 to make sure my bag made it onto the airplane, and another $10 to gain entrance to the VIP waiting area.

When I got through to the waiting area, an airport employee who did not speak English, snatched up my passport and tickets. I followed his back to the end of the corridor where he disappeared around the corner. I became nervous when I'd realized a half hour had passed and there was still no sign of the employee. I tried to remember what he looked like, in case I needed to identify him in a line up. Navy blue shirt, was it? To my relief, he returned, seconds before I panicked, handing me my stamped documents, and waving me off toward the waiting area. I was happy to learn that my patience and trust, albeit somewhat reluctant, paid off.

I completed my evaluation on the long flight home, feeling good about the project despite the critical situation. Congo is still very much a part of World Care's current agenda. I believe that World Care's multiple capabilities will help the community of Matadi's 300,000 residents over time. Now that the rebel forces are diminishing, and the territories they formerly occupied are fragmented, people are eager to rebuild, restore peace, and get on with their lives. With deep, lush jungles that fill the landscape and blanket millions of acres of land along the Nile and the Congo rivers, there is a promise of resources for growth that could come from the small humanitarian projects that remain. The women and children continue to encourage me to find hope in the desperate environment of the Congo.

After my return from the Congo, I felt overjoyed that I could continue working at the level that I once had, albeit with caution. Meanwhile, the U.S. and global economy had taken a turn for the worse. It was the spring of 2008. Gas prices were at an all time high at over four dollars per gallon. Additionally, food prices had doubled in less than a year, and the housing industry had plummeted to create a domino effect of epic proportions. As a result, countries overseas who usually supplied to America had to resort to food rationing, reducing exports to keep more goods circulating locally.

Humanitarian aid groups are overwhelmed by need requirements with tightened resources for distribution. Myanmar (formally Burma), recently experienced a massive cyclone that killed thousands, and Szechuan Province in China was devastated by an earthquake that killed over 20,000 people, and displaced over a million more. But, with the 2008 Olympics in sight, China, eager to burnish its image as the host of the Games, was reluctant to let anyone witness the devastation, let alone help to rebuild it.

Even though we serve our local community every day, more work and volunteers are always needed. But with hope and guidance from my dreams, World Care and the people who share a similar vision are here to lend a hand. As I move forward in life, my mission is to continue to search for truth and help others with the gifts that God has given me.

My dreams continue to guide as well as warn of obstacles I may face.

Afterward

World Care's path is for them – for the women and children who have suffered unconscionably for as long as humans have existed - plain and simple. Entire nations and religions have devoted their existence to the oppression of women, thus stunting the growth of humanity, and creating the need for organizations like World Care to come in, bring aid and rebuild hope for the impoverished and oppressed. World Care exists for those who have endured rape, genital mutilation in the name of God, slavery, physical abuse, mental abuse, beatings, shootings, experiments, torture and massacres.

I work for people who have suffered and still have the strength left to go on living. Our modest efforts to restore basic human rights allow us to reach, educate, and give a little more hope to alleviate human suffering. We can never become complacent in our efforts, no matter how corrupt and impossible a situation may seem. Even a small effort can amount to big changes. We must never stop fighting for justice, respect, and equality for all human beings. My humble role is to ensure that World Care can continue to expand and answer that calling.

Despite having traveled around the world to many dangerous, war-torn countries, I count riding in a cab in New York to be among my most frightening experiences to date. Each time, there's a new cab driver faster than the last, each time a new set of obstacles - a parade, an overheated bus, or a pack of aggressive cyclists, you name it – along the way to the stillness of my hotel room. On a recent trip to New York, in the spring of 2008, I braced myself for another death-defying ride.

As I stepped off of the elevators to the exit at Grand Central station, I joined the line to wait for my latest death cab. When it got to be my turn, I stepped up to the cab and opened the door. I nearly gasped out loud when I caught sight of the driver. He looked like an overgrown hippie who hadn't bathed in months, the mere sight of him warned of the worst smells you could imagine and I hadn't even caught a whiff yet. There was a look in his eyes like he wanted to kill or eat me or something, a crazed look any way you slice it. I looked back at the long line of people still awaiting their way home. I took a breath of city air, and ducked into the cab.

I gave the driver my hotel address and braced myself for the worst. The sudden stops and turns were to be expected but combined with the pair of eyes in the rear view mirror, they jolted me even more. I started a conversation with the guy mostly so I'd quit holding my breath. His comments and answers were all a little wacky, like he was on drugs or else recovering from a hangover, or maybe even still drunk. His driving was not impaired, according to the extremely low standards for cab drivers I'd come to know. He was just kind of out there, and it was unsettling. Talking to him made the ride less uncomfortable, but only slightly.

"So are you from here?" I thought he was on a Bluetooth cell phone but he was actually just talking to himself. I repeated, "So are you from here, New York?"

"Oh, oh yeah, I am."

I think he was stunned that I was talking to him. He began telling me about the history of New York and the buildings. He was quite articulate and well versed in history as he spoke about the land and companies like Dutch East India Company that founded the city in the 1600's.

The conversation moved to Ground Zero. I wasn't sure if I should mention my involvement with World Care and our experiences in the aftermath of 9/11; I wasn't sure how he'd react. Instead, I asked him if he knew what was happening with the construction efforts. I had heard that the possibility of rebuilding the towers was one option, as was creating a memorial park. As we neared my destination, he told me that he wasn't sure if any decisions had been made, somewhat slurring his words. I noticed a drop of saliva trickling down his chin. Yes, he was that creepy.

Then the strangest thing happened. He turned his head to look back at me and asked, "Did you know that before the towers were built, the area was used as a land fill?" At that moment time stopped, this new information about Ground Zero was paralyzing. My jaw dropped into my lap. I was the one with drool running down my chin now. We arrived at my destination. Still shocked, I paid the driver and collected my bags. I watched the cab speed off, half expecting it to disappear into thin air. Life's messages come in unusual packages sometimes.

I thought back to my dream in 1998, foreshadowing the events from 9/11.

The buildings falling down in clouds of venomous smoke. The Middle Eastern man at the wheel of the car, pushing buttons on a black panel, in rhythm with the destruction. His license plate. A Green Bay Packers plate holder. The plate read: Land Fil.

A Note from the Author

Dear Readers,

I am grateful to be able to go on working in the same capacity with nominal limitation. My journey so far has brought me a sense of contentment, truth, and understanding of how humanity works. If I have learned anything, I have learned that dreams, freedom, humility, love, and life are gifts. They are to be cherished and respected and oftentimes fought for. You don't have to go to the other side of the world to see pain. We all have our own struggles and we can see the suffering around us, or at least read about it, on a daily basis. Witnessing atrocities creates a severe mental burden, but that burden should never be forgotten because it provides a valuable reference point from which to model our own lives. Despite countless successes, there is still much room for improvement, especially for families and children living in the darkest corners of the earth, searching for light every day of their lives. We all have the ability to act; my hope is that each of us finds our unique inner purpose, that which empowers us to create change for a better world.

If you feel inspired by this story and would like to make a contribution to the organization, or would like to learn more about World Care, please go to *www.worldcare.org*. Your support is greatly needed and appreciated.

Lisa M. Hopper

About the Author

World Care, started in Lisa Hopper's garage in 1994, is the culmination of decades of professional experience and remarkable observations, and illustrates her compassion, leadership, insight, and broad international exposure. World Care International has collected and redirected over 30,663,739 pounds of resources valued at over $40 million dollars to aid in humanitarian efforts worldwide, to date. All of this has been accomplished with less than 3% of its annual funds going to administration, making it one of the most efficient non-profit organizations in the country.

Hopper's success in helping people, her resourcefulness, and organizational genius have not been ignored. Her accolades include: Global Visionary Award 2009, *National Points of Light Award*, YWCA *Women on the Move*, Ernst and Young *Award for Business Leadership*, J.C. Penney Company *Golden Rule* for Outstanding Service in Education, *Governor's Pride in Arizona* for Distinguished Community Achievement, *Karen McQuillan Award*, Corporate Volunteer Council's *Outstanding Volunteer Service*, Mexican Federal Congress *International Humanitarian Relief*, Optimist International *Achievement in Education*, Volunteer Center of Tucson *World Class Volunteer*, Rotary Club of Guatemala *Outstanding Recognition*, Tucson Citizen *Volunteer Of The Year*, and *Dynamic Duo Award*.

Lisa Hopper is currently CEO and Founder of World Care, an adjunct lecturer at the University of Arizona Honors College in International Studies and Social Entrepreneurism, and has been an international consultant on concessions negotiations to a multitude of foreign countries. She is an Honorary Commander alumnus for the 355th Aerospace Medical Squadron at Davis-Monthan Air Force Base, and is the Emergency Relief Chair for

LULAC International Disaster response. She currently resides at the base of the Santa Catalina Mountains in Tucson, Arizona.